TRANSACTIONAL ANALYSIS

IN

MANAGEMENT

By

Julie Hewson
and
Colin Turner

Published by The Staff College

ISBN 0 90 7659 77 2

© The Staff College 1992

Published by The Staff College
Coombe Lodge
Blagdon
Bristol, BS18 6RG
Tel (0761) 462503
Fax (0761) 463140

Typesetting by Action Typesetting, Gloucester
Printed in the UK by Booksprint, Bristol

Cartoons by Susan Leather, The Staff College
Layout and sub-editing by Pippa Toogood, The Staff College

CONTENTS

LIST OF FIGURES

INTRODUCTION

Transactional analysis (TA) has been wonderfully effective in the process of change and development in many areas of human experience. Outstandingly, it has been successful in the area of psychotherapy. It has been a potent model and tool that therapists have employed in their work with individual clients or groups of clients. Many people have found that even without the help of therapists, transactional analysis has brought illumination and understanding into their lives, and helped them make new choices about the kinds of people they want to be and where they want to go.

TA has, however, had nothing like such a powerful impact on the world of work and work organisations. It has been incorporated into some training schemes for staff, particularly for the purpose of improving client or customer relationships; and many managers will have had at least a fleeting encounter with the concept of organisational games. Compared with the depth and intensity of work at the personal therapy level however, it hardly begins to register. Whereas the vigour of intellectual thinking that has gone on for many years in the psychotherapy aspect of TA is impressive, there is little to parallel that in areas of organisation theory, organisation behaviour or management studies. There are some notable exceptions such as Julie Hay, Michael Reddy and David Barker. At least a part of this may be because most of the leading transactional analysts over the last two decades have been independently employed psychotherapists whose work is primarily with individuals, and whose working lives do not take place within work organisations, as the term is typically understood. Of course, all people earning a living from TA have to organise themselves, sometimes in co-operation or partnership with other like-minded people, but this is a qualitatively different experience from working in factories, offices, schools, banks, colleges, insurance companies, department stores and the like. This is not a criticism. Most people are likely to be infinitely more interested in their own development than that of their work organisation. But the latter has its importance too. Many people spend much of their lives in them, and they deserve their share of study.

We, the authors, are enthusiastic about applying TA to the work organisation. We have made our contribution in writing this book, and in running a series of conferences on TA and management, but we hope that many more people will bring their talent, insight and creativity to this area of applied TA.

We have chosen to set the scene in an educational organisation, a post-16 college, but it is very simply transposed to the school setting, and with little more effort to the commercial or industrial company. As a collaborating work team our experiences and training complement each other well.

Julie is a highly trained transactional analyst who holds clinical qualifications and works as a psychotherapist running her own training centre. Until 1987 she worked as a full-time member of staff in a large arts and technology college. Julie has also worked as a management consultant in education and industry.

Colin is a management trainer and consultant, also specialising in organisation theory, who worked full-time at The Staff College until 1991. He has also been involved with the TA movement from its earliest years in this country and has introduced it into many Staff College courses.

Between the two of us, we feel we balance well.

The fact that we have both now chosen to work freelance indicates the problem of keeping even interested people like ourselves actually within a work organisation. So we write this book now while our experiences are very recent.

There was a third person involved in the writing of this book, Pippa Andrews. Though formally employed as the editor, she took full part in all the formative discussions, adding her ideas and putting ours through critical evaluation. Her influence is strong on the final outcome.

Our thanks are due to Susan Leather who provided the illustrations and designed the cover.

Pippa Toogood managed the project through its various processes from first scripts to the finished book. Along the way she raised many queries on the text which helped us avoid error or improve the coherence and clarity of the writing. For all of that, we thank her.

The book is written primarily for people working in management roles. In the culture of colleges and schools, management roles are spread widely through the staff, and we see this book as being helpful to those at all levels.

The first part describes a college and some of the management activities that took place in it. It is a fictional case study, and the behaviour of the managers and staff is used to highlight key concepts in TA.

The second part of the book consists of support chapters to the first part. It contains explanatory chapters on the main concepts of TA, including some which are very specific to TA in organisations. We believe it is helpful to think of it this way round – the experience is primary, and to make sense of that it may be necessary to refer to the theoretical support system. However, we would encourage readers to use the book in whatever way fits their needs best, and it is certainly no disadvantage to read the theoretical section first.

Section One: Management in Practice

Chapter 1
Trentwood Technical College

The college lay on a dual carriageway and was most commonly seen from the other side of the road, looming over the streams of traffic going to or from the town centre. Visitors on foot had to walk a hundred yards down to the traffic lights to cross the road, or rely on agility and speed to reach the concrete raised barrier that separated the two streams of traffic, then make a further dash to reach the pavement and front door of the college. The long college frontage consisted of brick and regularly spaced metal framed windows, painted cream. It could have been just another of the many light engineering or food processing factories built along this artery in the '30s and '50s, were it not for the pseudo-impressive central entrance. This was a portico surrounded by steps leading to the massive front door, one half of which was permanently locked. When the college was built in 1938 it had been thought a very grand building, an expression of civic pride, which was reflected in the commemorative stone to the side of the door, recording the official opening and, more importantly, the official opener.

Any grandeur disappeared once through the door, for internally the building, which was very shallow for all its façade, was dreary. The corridors were narrow, the classrooms standard school rooms and the large hall immediately opposite the entrance had all the squalor of a room with the eating habits and needs of young people in mind, because the architects had only ever designed schools before.

Most visitors, staff and students never entered the front door, nor indeed this part of the building. Motorists drove past the college if coming out of town, past the traffic lights to a large roundabout and turned back on the other side to a large traffic island. They then turned into a side street just before the college grounds, and via that negotiated a way into the back of the college to one of the three car parks. These had been created, and were a godsend at the time, when some small factories had been demolished, and the space still had the feel of derelict ground. Walking from the car park meant negotiating your way between temporary huts of various vintages and materials, but with good luck the first-time visitor would reach the main college building, a late '60s, five-storey block of windows and faded blue panels. A quirk of the architects had aligned this building obliquely to the original '30s building and the huts, so that the effect was a random placing of all the parts. However, the tower block was not a bad building, as such buildings go.

On the opposite side of the road was the former college of art, now the Trentwood Technical College School of Art. It was a considerable contrast. Standing in matured grounds, the fine Edwardian villa comprised the main part of the school. A modern extension to the back had been sensitively designed to provide an aesthetically pleasing and functional building which won an award for its architects. Most of the art school's staff referred to the main college site as a modern slum and visited it as seldom as possible.

The environment of the main college was not particularly attractive. There were few trees and no flowers, and the usual detritus of used coke tins, chip and sweet papers, cigarette ends and more bizarre items, accumulated in whatever corner the wind tended to blow them. Not all was dismal however. The arrival of a new principal, Alison Mapp, a few months earlier had marked the start of serious attention to improving the public face of the college. She had already instigated two valuable changes. Bright and clear signs had appeared throughout the college and grounds so that for the first time in the college's history there was a reasonable presumption that visitors could find the part of the college they actually wanted. If they went to the reception area in the tower building, they would find a cheerful foyer with welcoming messages, indoor plants and an open desk staffed by professionally trained receptionists. Gone were the green tubular canvas chairs and the glass window which effectively denied the enquirer access to any attention. Tacky notices sellotaped onto doors or windows had been removed, and pictures, bright posters, and well printed notices had replaced them.

The college had steadily expanded its services to the public. Courses were provided in most of the major vocational areas: engineering, construction, hairdressing, business studies, arts and crafts, social work, plus a wide variety of general education courses which attracted students from across the city. Its reputation, as in most colleges, varied from excellent to poor depending on whom you asked. The college was not immune from the problems besetting all further education at this time. There was rivalry with a local sixth form centre. Adult education was mostly preserved in separate institutes and no one yet knew the effects of a recently founded city college of technology. Local financial delegation, relationships with the new Training and Enterprise Councils (TECs), a declining 16 year old age group, and more general concerns about the effect of EC changes in 1993 and of possible requirements to implement quality standards based on BS 5750, ensured that those in management positions could take home their fair share of the executive burden.

This is the college that Alison Mapp had recently embraced as her new work home. We will see in the following pages how she met and engaged with her colleagues. She had been told at her interview that this was a friendly college. Was it really turning out to be so? She had been told that this was a college with a new vision for the future where exciting things were going to happen, and she was lucky to be in at the start of this brave new enterprise. Was she really finding that was how it was? A part of her was excited and pleased that she had won the appointment over her competitors. A part of her was committed to the general direction which the governing body had indicated. Yet another part of her was sceptical about what really went on in the daily life of the college. She had enough experience in her former colleges to know that sexism, poor management, racism and low morale were rampant in many places that presented a flattering image to the outside world.

Alison's predecessor had been a dour ex-RAF officer, whose specialism had been mechanical engineering and who viewed the college as a machine comprised of pieces that had to fit together in order to function effectively. Each part worked, some more effectively than others, but there was little understanding between departments of what each did or how the parts comprised the whole. When Alison arrived, from a business studies background and a specialism in economics and marketing, she felt she had come to head a group of self-governing villages who didn't even speak the same language, whose dress customs and values were different, and who rarely sought to 'trade' with each other.

Into this college walked, on a Monday morning in September, Frazer Brown, the newly appointed head of department. He had moved from a large college in a provincial town. Prior to that, he had been involved in youth and community work, where he had been extremely active in setting up a number of creative projects for young people who had been in care. He arrived at the college full of enthusiasm, ideas and political fire.

As Frazer Brown entered his new workplace, he was beset by the uncertainty and inner questioning that came from a part of him that he hadn't listened to for a while – not since the first day of his last post, or further back still, his first day at university. Alongside the excitement of a new setting, new people to meet and a new challenge was the anxious voice, stifled under collar and tie, asking the irritating questions in a plaintive tone: Will I be accepted? Will they like me? Will there really be a place for me? Will I have to fight for my position here? How much rivalry is there between existing members? Is this a healthy, happy place to be in? What are the unwritten rules? Am I going to break them?

This is a normal process that few people talk about and is in many ways reminiscent of our entry into our family of origin, our first day at school and a number of other new beginnings. In this situation the Archaic Child ego state is likely to be activated and old memories, feelings and expectations may be lurking just below the surface. Alison had felt much the same four months earlier.

Within the college there was very little sense of bonding between departments. Each part went its own way with a nod in the direction of other members but little real contact. The story of the birth of the organisation gives us a clue as to why this has happened.

Originally there was a technical college specialising in engineering, building trades, secretarial courses, and courses on bookkeeping, catering and hairdressing, housed in a utility building. A few hundred yards away an architect-designed, prestigious edifice combined with the Edwardian villa, housed the art college. Students from the two institutions saw little in common with each other, as did the staff. Then, at the stroke of a pen in County Hall the two institutions were amalgamated! There followed the addition of academic subjects – A levels and the like. Then came travel and tourism, business studies and management training, community care, cartography, fashion design, computer courses and fine furniture making. Each of these additions felt like an unwanted pregnancy to the original technical college staff, though they would have been most unlikely to attach such a label to their disquiet. The art school, which had somehow managed to maintain its separateness and self-prestige, began to feel inexorably sucked into a college with proliferating departments. In material terms there was great anxiety about whether there would be enough to go around despite the fact that the budget had increased with the size of the college.

Frazer had come to head a newly formed department, hived off from catering and hairdressing and now resplendent under the name of Health and Community Care Services. It was located in an annexe. Frazer experienced a sense of fragmentation about the college without fully understanding why. It was only later that he discovered the historical background to the place. Thus he, along with the other heads of department, took what seemed the only option – to focus his attention on his own department and endeavour to make that work.

Arriving at 8.15 on his first morning he was greeted by his secretary, a capable, efficient woman in her late 50s, elegant in dress and overall appearance and who smoked like a train – Frazer was a non-smoker! Gradually the staff filtered in and Frazer had a peculiar sensation of having become foster parent to a bunch of rather disgruntled and, under the surface, rebellious kids who had been kicked off the main site into a cold, forlorn annexe on the outskirts of town. Two of them had applied for the head of department post. One of these was now being extremely helpful, the other was throwing cynical comments about the place, such as, 'Wait till you've been here as long as I have.' No chance, thought Frazer. There were three dedicated lecturers in their late 40s concerned with training youngsters who wished to enter the caring professions, three who had worked in social services in varying capacities, two catering specialists, a craft lecturer, a nursing specialist, a physical education lecturer, a few other non-specialists who could turn their hands to anything (some successfully, others not so), two technicians, two secretaries and 17 part-timers. How was he to bond this lot into a team?

The three care studies lecturers were demonstrating the same strategy that Frazer had decided to adopt at departmental level *vis à vis* the college. They, however, had elected to do so at course level, *vis à vis* the department. They made it abundantly clear in the first staff meeting that they were not interested in departmental politics. What they wanted was to concentrate on their courses and their students.

In the systems model of transactional analysis, on which some of this book is based (see chapter 18), one of the most important processes that determines the basis on which the individual grows is the initial bonding, dependency relationship. This is also true in organisations. Current organisational consultants using transactional analysis emphasise the importance of the individual bonding with the organisation, meaning by that a sense of belonging, of having a valued part to play, a sense of identification. In industry it is sometimes referred to as a corporate identity. What was clear to Frazer was that this was not in evidence at the college level and its absence had filtered down to departmental level. Nobody seemed to have a true sense of belonging except in small units here and there, and in the art school which still saw itself as a separate entity. [1]

The next problem the new head of department had to address was how to give and receive quality attention. In transactional analysis language this is referred to as stroking. This word was chosen by Eric Berne, the originator of transactional analysis, because our initial experience of attention when we were new born was through the quality of the physical contact. This later becomes transformed into other symbols of appreciation – pay rises, promotion, written thanks, criticism. Strokes can be positive or negative. They can also be conditional or unconditional (i.e. for doing or being respectively). Chapter 8 describes strokes in more detail.

Some people have a preference for verbal strokes. They like to be told how they are doing; they like to give praise. Others prefer to use non-verbal

---

[1] At one college this problem was addressed by the new principal who, within a few months of arriving, instigated training days for senior members from each department which he ran himself. These days were fun, focused on team building and provided a vehicle by which people who had worked in the same college for a number of years finally got to meet each other. Through this a bonding across departments began to have roots which was later built upon through the creation of inter-disciplinary marketing teams. The principal also put himself on the line and came across as a person, not just a role.

strokes such as sending a card on an important occasion, buying a colleague a drink at lunchtime, making sure that what he or she has ordered is expedited. Touch is the third way of stroking and needs to be used with some degree of caution in the workplace.

In an organisation where people are appreciated for their skills, contribution and dedication, there is a healthy sense of personal value and commitment. Most of us like to believe that we matter, that we are valued and that what we do well is noticed. In Trentwood College stroking was a bit hit and miss. In fact, what was done went largely unacknowledged – that's what you are paid to do, was the unspoken norm. But should something go wrong then the mistake was given plenty of attention (of the negative variety). The greatest dispenser of negative strokes was one of the vice-principals, who blocked any creative initiative, and who was seen by others as placing great importance on showing how paperwork should be done or how forms were not being filled in correctly. The result of this lack of positive stroking was a degree of cynicism and world-weariness on the part of lecturing staff, for any memo that 'came from above'. Some staff got their strokes from the performance and gratitude of their students. Others regularly had 'Wilting'[2] experiences with 'Meat 1' or their equivalent, where negative stroking was the cultural currency. This mixed stroking environment further added to the fragmentation. This was manifested in the fabric of the different departments' buildings. Some looked quite inviting, others very neglected and dishevelled. Alison's heart had sunk on her tour of the campus during her first two weeks in college. The worst places had not been shown to her during her interview.

Frazer found very little stroking between his staff, lots between staff and students and a depressing, ugly environment.

Claude Steiner (Steiner, 1974) talks about what he describes as the Stroke Economy, which is a belief that there are not enough positive strokes to go around – a competitive philosophy based on scarcity. This is maintained, he says, by a series of unwritten rules which, if followed, lead to a loveless, joyless existence. These rules are: don't give strokes (i.e. don't pass remarks); don't accept strokes (i.e. the nice ones which show you have an inflated sense of self); don't reject strokes (i.e. the critical ones – they are supposed to be good for you); don't ask for strokes (people are supposed to read minds); and don't give yourself strokes (that's just plain selfish)!

Frazer decided to set about systematically breaking each one of these rules. First he had his office redecorated and moved into a smaller room (one of the perks of being in an annexe) while it was being done. He bought plants for the foyer and indented for decorative work throughout the building. He

---

[2] Tom Sharpe's book **Wilt** (Sharpe, 1978) is a fund of interesting transactions.

asked for creative displays from the art department, and liaised with the part of the college which ran painting and decorating courses to give students something to get their teeth into. This had an additional, unforeseen bonus in that it created a balance of the sexes in the isolated annexe, as his department comprised mainly female students.

Next, he had an interview with each of his staff members at which he really listened to what they had to say. He asked for their opinions, ignored or rejected destructive or gratuitous criticism and encouraged positive problem solving and strategic thinking. He found out the strengths of his staff and stroked those strengths. Prior to any staff development interview, which was to come later, he began asking what each member of staff most wanted to achieve in the next 12 months.

To begin with, some of the staff were cynical and filtered out the positive strokes or turned them into negatives ('What's he after?' they asked themselves).

Others were more ready to accept positive strokes and began to feel a sense of value and belonging. Colleagues who more readily accepted strokes began to risk giving them to others and even though the cynics still bantered, their criticism began to take on a more humorous tone; so that even they, despite themselves, sometimes found themselves giving the occasional positive stroke.

Frazer had no students to teach and had to be careful not to be seen to favour one of his lecturing staff at the expense of others, though naturally he had his preferences. This was quite hard because it tended to keep him isolated. He gradually developed a companionable relationship with his secretary as long as she didn't smoke in his office.

What became increasingly clear was that staff needed different strokes for different ego states. This and the following concepts in this section are more fully discussed in chapter 6. Suffice here to say that Berne (borrowing from his mentor Paul Federn who talked about varying states of the ego) created the term 'ego states' to refer to different states of being, feeling, thinking and behaving. He gave them three names; the Archaic Child, the Integrated Adult and the Introjected Parent ego states – Child, Adult and Parent for short. The Child and the Parent are both historical parts of our personality, while the Adult is the one that functions in relation to the immediate environment.

Sometimes a member of staff would appear in Frazer's office a bit like a child might; sometimes distressed, sometimes rebellious, sometimes bewildered (Child ego state). At other times that same member of staff might come feeling affronted, furious or concerned about a specific incident (Parent ego state). At other times he would come with a planned strategy to enable, for example, a submission for a new course to proceed (Adult ego state). Each of these aspects of the personality or ego states needed different kinds of stroking.

Frazer realised that some of his staff needed their Parent ego state stroked. These were the ones with very firms beliefs – 'ought' and 'should' figured heavily in their conversations – who always 'meant well'. They were extremely dedicated but often infuriated the more pragmatic or intellectual staff members who experienced them as believing they had a monopoly of the truth. The staff with a very active Parent ego state always knew what was best, assumed everyone in their right mind would see things their way and cut across any analytical discussion with impatience. Frazer had to avoid being overwhelmed by some of these who were only too willing to teach him his job, and while stroking the positive aspects of their Parent ego state, encouraged them to be aware of different frames of reference. In the language of transactional analysis this would mean to invite them into their Adult ego state.

Others might only come to Frazer when the Child in them was in distress. They might want, above all, to be heard and have a place to let off steam, before they felt ready to engage their Adult and plan a strategy to deal with a problem.

Yet other staff would keep their private selves out of any interaction with the 'boss' and come to him only to deal with current matters. They left Frazer in no doubt that any stroking that went beyond the boundaries of the role and the job in hand would be totally unacceptable. They carried their Child home with them at night and took unresolved difficulties out on the garden, the cat or themselves.

He found it most difficult to deal with staff who consistently seemed to come from a Child position. He was not their father or their old headmaster, but somehow felt he was being forced into that role. He then discovered the four ways of diagnosing ego states.

- Phenomenologically when you feel just like a teenager or a seven year old;
- historically when you remember what is was like when you first went to school;
- socially when you respond in a way that has been invited by the other person, e.g. like a headmaster (perhaps one modelled on your experience);
- behaviourally when you notice things about a person's tone of voice, or body language and posture that are indicative of an authoritarian approach (Parent), rebelliousness (Child) or thoughtful and questioning mode (Adult).

Behaviour that is not congruent with the current situation may be an indication of how, historically, the person defended him or herself in a traumatic situation.

What is very clear from the work of Eric Berne is that our current sense of self is often influenced by the 'psychic presence' (Berne 1975) of parental figures.

Although the person may not be relating to current reality, he or she may be actually experiencing what is happening with the perceptual, emotional, intellectual and social capacities of the child at the time of repression and fixation. (Erskine 1991)

In becoming aware of the transactional patterns and the ego states from which they come, we can become more highly attuned to some of the external (extero-psychic) and old (archeo-psychic) elements that can influence interactional patterns (Berne 1975); and of the Integrated Adult (neo-psyche) which accounts for and integrates what is occuring now in the internal and external environment.

CHAPTER 2
TIME FOR HEADS OF DEPARTMENT

As Alison walked into the Monday heads of department meeting it was with a surprising air of foreboding. How was she going to meld this disparate group of people and departments into a working entity? She glanced around the room at small groups having the ritual cup of coffee and pastiming, talking about the weekend, plans for the future, holidays and in-house gossip. There was Frazer Brown, the new head of department from Community Services talking to Carmella Armaroso from Business Studies. Harry Jones from Engineering was already waiting to start, with his papers in front of him. Austin Graves, from Building, just entering the room, went to sit beside him. In the far corner in earnest conversation stood Lali Singh who was in charge of Sport and Recreation, John Eccles (Catering and Hairdressing), Geraldine Masters (vice-principal responsible for curriculum) and Steve Yates (vice-principal responsible for resources).

We are still waiting for Bill and Mary, thought Alison, and I really ought to bring this meeting to order.

'Let's begin,' she said. 'I know Bill's external examiners for the Fine Arts Diploma have arrived so he might be a little late. Has anyone seen Mary Woods?' (Mary was Head of Academic and Social Studies.)

There was very little information amongst the murmers.

'Would you all take your seats so we can begin? Today's meeting is specifically designed to address quality,' said Alison, moving people out of **pastiming** and into **activities**. Activities are goal directed, whereas pastiming is a way of exchanging strokes in a familiar, non-threatening way, usually about something that has happened in the past or might happen in the future, e.g. discussing the group, each other or events, participating in chat but engaging in no action concerning it.

'You know that one of our agreed plans this year is to look at quality assurance within the college, and to look at areas where change is needed. To this end, as our first point of discussion, I am suggesting bringing in a group of outside consultants. Their names are Harding and Hawkins.'

'Quite right,' Harry Jones (Engineering) looked up, 'I think it is high time that we looked at some standards round here. Our lads have very clear performance criteria on our courses. It's what industry expects.'

'What we need to address is hard, objective data,' Steve Yates interposed. 'Exam results across departments, cost per student, number of contact hours per course, then we'll know where we stand.'

At that point Mary Woods entered the room. 'I'm sorry I'm late, important phone call. What's this about cost per student and exam results?'

'We are talking about quality assurance throughout the college.'

'Surely we're here for students to have real education and improved learning. It's a negation of educational philosophy to measure everything in terms of exam results. We're getting closer and closer to training criteria and further and further away from the reasons many of us entered this field.'

'It's the way everything is going,' said Carmella.

'Well I don't like it and my department can't be measured in those terms,' said Mary.

'What makes your department so special?' snapped Austin Graves. 'We are in the business of education just as much as you are.'

Frazer Brown watched, surprised and dumbfounded, as people began to take up 'not-OK' positions on the Drama Triangle. So far the positions filled were that of Persecutor and Victim.

John Eccles came in next. 'I'm sure we all feel we're involved in both education and training,' (thus filling the third role in the drama triangle, that of Rescuer).

'Don't speak for me, speak for yourself,' said Carmella. 'I can't stand it when people say 'we' when they mean 'I'.' (Persecutor)

This series of transactions, familiar as they are, are the beginnings of a **game**. Games always entail some kind of discount of self, others or options and lead, through a process of exchanges, to a point where things seem to switch. The people involved begin to wonder what is going on, and the whole thing ends with bad feelings all round. During the process there is a series of secret messages (ulterior transactions) and the bad feelings at the end are described as the pay-off (see chapter 12 on Games).

At that moment Bill Tyson, head of the art school, came in. He helped himself to a coffee and in a whisper to Geraldine asked what had happened so far. He then smiled at Alison, tendered his apologies and said: 'The art school has had nationally acclaimed results for the past five years. I don't think we need to be concerned about quality. Our students win prizes all over the place.'

'My concern,' said Frazer Brown, cutting across, 'is how do you find out the quality of what is really going on?'

'That's the reason for calling in Harding and Hawkins. They are experts in this field,' replied Alison.

'Experts be damned. We are the experts here in this college, we know what is needed by the various examining boards or industry. Why pay an arm and a leg to get so-called experts in? We could spend the money on something more useful, like the laser printer I've been on about for the Travel and Tourism course,' said Carmella with vigour.

Lali Singh sat back in his chair thinking of the performance of La Traviata he had seen the previous weekend. As he sat there musing he was in **withdrawal,** another way of structuring time, where people disassociate themselves from what is going on around them and retreat into themselves, often finding good sources of strokes, feelings, memories and fantasies. Alternatively they may start worrying about things outside the current situation, thus experiencing bad feelings when the current reality would not be a source of negativism.

'I think,' said Frazer, 'that first of all we need to think about what quality assurance means to our individual departments and the courses that we are offering, and then go on to look at the college as a whole. This is what we are really leading to isn't it? Bringing together our disparate departments and somehow developing a kind of corporate identity that has some meaning?'

Here our new member of staff is confronting what is known as the ulterior or psychological message. One of the problems in the college was fragmentation; most heads of department wanted to maintain the status quo. Probably only a new mind could pick up the resistance with such clarity.

Smart arse, thought Austin Graves, and said: 'That sounds like sense.'

'I propose we use the rest of the meeting time to analyse individual criteria for quality that directly relate to your courses and departments, and then get back together for the last half hour to brainstorm some ideas about quality assurance for the whole college. Let's say 45 minutes on your own,' said Alison.

'I think that's a good idea, are we agreed?' asked Geraldine.

'If I'd known this is what we were going to do I could have spent more time with the external examiner and done this later. After all, that's about quality assurance too you know,' said Bill.

'I think,' said Alison, ignoring this hook, 'that what we need to do first is define our terms. What do we mean by quality assurance? If you would spend a few minutes in sub-groups discussing what you understand by quality assurance, we could all start from the same nominative level at least. By that, I mean,' she stopped herself from catching someone's eye,'that we can explore and come to some agreement about what the name quality assurance means for each of us as individuals, and as a team.'

As her colleagues shifted their chairs to address this, Alison called Frazer over.

'Well, what do you think?' She smiled up at him.

He grinned back at her, 'It's amazing how clearly you can see into a process when you are outside it. Being new can sometimes be an advantage.

I am sure I would have been just as myopic in my last college. When you put a lot of energy into building up a department, you're not very keen to dilute it in any way. Talking about quality in terms of the college as a whole might feel like that for some people. Others like Harry seem to be really getting their teeth into it.'

'Thanks,' said Alison.

This exchange is known as **intimacy,** where there is a real and deep meeting between two people, sometimes in shared perceptions, as in this case, sometimes in anger, sometimes with love or affection.

In any meeting or group, individual members will probably structure the time in a variety of ways. Each of these ways has a function for the individual and for the group as a whole (see chapter 13 on Time structuring).

In Alison's heads of department meeting **withdrawal** was seen when individual members either physically or psychologically absented themselves from what was going on in the meeting, e.g. Lali Singh thinking about the opera.

Rituals are predictable, well prescribed activities that lead to strokes of minimum risk, and set the scene for further encounters, in this case having coffee before the meeting. Other people will have a special seat they occupy on the commuter train every morning, a regular greeting, or a joke.

Pastiming is the exchange of 'abouts', i.e. talking about things outside the current context – holidays, other people etc. It also includes those ways of passing the time – visits to the pub, coffee mornings, and so on. They are a source of attention (strokes) and a way of getting to know people with a view to deciding who you'd like to get to know better. As a social tool, this process can act as a way of sampling a range of people with a view to getting to know some more intimately. At work, it can be a way of avoiding 'getting down to business'.

Activities are goal directed ways of structuring time; for example, getting down to agenda items at a meeting, marking papers, teaching a class, putting up a shelf. It is also true that an activity can include within its scope other ways of structuring time; teaching a class, for example, can involve rituals, pastiming, activities, games and intimacy.

Games are repetitive patterns of behaviour which have the flavour of 'here we go again'. They start with some kind of undervaluing or minimising (discount) of self, others or options. They proceed with a series of ulterior transactions and are characterised by an unexpected shift or switch where people involved suddenly experience surprise, confusion or irritation. Then they are followed by a pay-off (some kind of bad feeling, e.g. irritation and annoyance and an internal dialogue that says, 'I don't know why I bother to come to these meetings, the whole thing is decided beforehand anyhow, nobody ever listens to me').

intimacy

ritual

withdrawal

activity

pastiming

Alison had some knowledge of what drove her colleagues. Each of them had qualities she valued and each endowed their perceptions with a subtly different emphasis which led to differing strategies when looking for solutions to problems.

Carmella would get things moving fast, she had no interest in dithering around as she put it. She worked efficiently and fast and sometimes her staff complained that they could not keep up with her. However, under stress she would get into a 'Hurry Up' driver, and start physically and psychologically moving at top speed. She often experienced this as a spinning sensation, and in response tried to go faster, thus making matters worse.

Harry, on the other hand, with his neatly sharpened pencils took his time, valuing precision and accuracy. It was partly his nature and partly due to his engineering training. He had started life as a tool maker and jig designer, skills that required immense accuracy. He paid attention to detail and looked for the facts. When stressed he would become more and more pedantic and slow, and people around him, especially those with Hurry Up drivers would be driven to distraction. He was driven by the Be Perfect driver which led him to backtrack and check for accuracy to an almost obsessive degree.

Bill, in his own way, as head of the art school, shared much in common with Harry though they might not have been willing to acknowledge the fact. Bill too was a perfectionist, and often felt frustrated with what he perceived as woolliness in the other departments. He just wanted to get on and enable his students to do what they had always done and that was to give his department national recognition for the quality of its work, particularly in graphics and textiles. He wasn't interested in anything that might dilute this excellence and was sceptical about wasting time on college ideas of excellence when he had his set up already.

Mary Tyson wanted most of all to please her students and staff. She was very empathetic and had been an effective teacher in her time although she rarely had the opportunity to use those skills now. She cared deeply for education, by which she meant the education of the whole person, not just cramming skills or knowledge into them. On a good day Mary was a delight to have around. She dispensed strokes to people with a largesse that was quite staggering. She listened, had time for people, smiled a lot and was generally cheerful. However, under stress she would first try to please others more and more. When that failed she would do something that appeared out of character, which was very selfish, or she would give and give and give until she was emotionally drained and felt ill and disheartened. She was driven by the Please Me driver (which means please others not yourself). In its positive form it is the valuing of other people's feelings and wanting to give them pleasure, and be empathetic. In its negative manifestation it can lead to people being perceived as sugary, too nice and inauthentic. There can also be the vague feeling that the recipient will have to repay all that is being given.

Lali Singh was a strong, silent character. Nobody ever knew what he was feeling. He was pleasant to have around and didn't make many emotional demands on his colleagues. He was an enigma to Mary. He was the kind of person who would keep a very cool head in a crisis. However, under stress his facial muscles would tighten and he would distance himself from those around him. Lali was driven at those times by the Be Strong driver, partly conditioned by the culture of his parents and partly from some of his early experiences at school, where other children, not understanding his traditions, persecuted him under the guise of 'just having a bit of fun'.

Austin, like Mary, had the Please Me driver and was regularly described as an affable chap. He also tended to be subject to the Try Harder driver when things were going wrong, particularly with regard to paperwork. Try Harder is the reverse side of the positive quality of perseverance. When in his driver behaviour a lot of energy was tied up showing people how hard he tried but not always in delivering the goods. However, he didn't give up easily.

Alison Mapp knew she had the Be Strong driver. She preferred to soldier on on her own. She had an extreme dislike of being dependent on others and she also ascribed to high standards of excellence. This made delegation very difficult for her.

Frazer had a tendency to be driven by Please Me, Be Strong and Be Perfect drivers – depending on his ego state. His Parent had Please Me and Be Perfect as the major drivers, his Child had Be Strong and Be Perfect.

In any team, the positive values underlying driver behaviour can be greatly appreciated. The Please Me driver has as its underlying base the positive value of true empathy and sensitivity to others. It is only when a person believes that they are only OK if they are forever pleasing others that a good value becomes distorted and the person feels driven.

Similarly with the Be Perfect. In its positive manifestation there is an emphasis on high standards and accuracy, quality and attention to detail. In the driven form it becomes 'I'm only OK if I'm perfect' and the person may become fearful and obsessive about their work, appearance or performance.

Hurry Up people in their positive state can be efficient, fast thinking and acting, and will enjoy a challenge and working on their own at their own pace. Under stress they become driven by 'I'm only OK if I hurry up' and can feel fragmented, highly anxious about missing deadlines and may, physically or metaphorically, start spinning or freeze and shut down altogether.

The positive value underlying Try Harder is dogged perseverance. These people never give up. Like Robert the Bruce and the spider, if at first you don't succeed, try, try again. The implication here is eventual success. However, in the negative, driven form, completion is what is missing. A lot of energy goes into showing everyone how hard the Try Harder person is trying but the end result is often incompletion.

Be Strong in its positive form is clear stability under stress, a cool head when all around are losing theirs. When a person is in driver behaviour they tend to cut themselves off from their own feelings and the feelings of other people. More about drivers can be found in chapter 15.

Alison knew that unless she learned to appreciate the mix in these, her senior management team, she would find her ideas and proposals sabotaged. She knew she might irritate Carmella because Be Perfects often pace themselves more slowly than Hurry Ups. But she was aware that her temperamental style was faster than the other two Be Perfects in her team, so she hoped she could act as a bridge between Harry, Bill and Carmella.

CHAPTER 3
ALISON'S SCRIPT

Alison was taking stock of herself, looking back to her past and thinking about the future. She had been by most accounts very successful. Appointed vice-principal at 31 and principal at 35, she had achieved up to this point all the success she could imagine. In fact when she thought about it, success was more or less written into her life from the start. In her family, success, though it had to be worked for, was assumed to be inevitable.

She remembered when she was a child hearing a story about when she was born. Her mother was a minor novelist whose works were now almost totally forgotten, but her mother's aunt was a formidable woman who had been one of the leading suffragettes in the first two decades of the century, and Aunt Florence it was who came to inspect the new-born child. 'She's a true Mapp,' she exclaimed. 'Another one for the cause. You can tell she is going to be a writer.' Aunt Florence insisted that the child's proposed names be changed from Alison Helen to Sylvia, after her great friend Sylvia Pankhurst.

Her father had in fact slipped the 'Alison' back in as a second name when he had registered her and though the family had called her Sylvia through her childhood, her father always called her Ally. She remembered being puzzled at primary school by her surname. Her mother and father were called Mapp, but her father's parents were called Brown. She asked her mother about it, as she was encouraged always to ask if puzzled. Her mother explained that when they got married any couple could choose either to take the wife's or husband's surname, and they had chosen her name. This solved Alison's problem, though she could not find any of her friends whose parents had done the same thing.

When she went to university, she decided to call herself Alison, and had been known as that ever since. It was, she realised now, shortly after her father died, though she made no connection at the time, and was not sure there was one. She had just thought 'Sylvia' rather old-fashioned.

Right through her childhood, which she remembered as a happy time, her relatives and parents paid much attention to her. At the time she just took it for granted that elders spent time playing quiz and word games, reading to her, listening to her reading and playing music, and telling her stories. Most of the games were in the form of competitions, and she was encouraged to enter outside competitions for writing poems and the like as well. She had no brothers or sisters, and though she occasionally played with other children outside school, she spent most of her time with adults. They certainly encouraged her a lot. She can remember often hearing one or the other say, 'You are a clever girl,' or 'You are going to be a real success,' and other little sayings such as 'Always aim for the stars,' 'Don't ask other people to do it – have a go yourself,' 'Stand up for yourself,' 'Never be satisfied with a shoddy job,' 'Keep asking, keep finding out.' She realised now how much time her mother and aunts had spent in answering her stream of questions and encouraging her to ask more.

Not surprisingly she had been a very bright child at primary school, effectively having intensive home tuition as well as excellent schoolteachers. She had been excited by the whole world opening up in front of her, though sometimes she felt sad when, as often happened, the other children went off to play, leaving her on her own. She never had a particular childhood friend, although she invented a few to talk to, but as her mother explained, most children were not gifted as she was and so could afford the luxury of playing around without doing anything in particular. Alison realised now that she had sometimes looked down on other children, thinking them stupid or childish, but she ruefully thought that she must have appeared to them as a real prig.

She went to a direct grant girls' school by scholarship, and carried on with her successful school career, ending up with an open scholarship to Oxford. She received much encouragement from the school staff and of course her family. At grammar school she developed her talent for woodwind playing and was also a fair tennis player and sprinter. She made one or two friends, and there were many more at this school who were not unlike her in attitude, but through her adolescence she quite often found herself feeling very lonely and depressed. She believed that she was not one of the people others really like, that she was not attractive to others in manner or appearance, and this made her feel very much on her own. She had plenty of resources to cope with these bouts of loneliness and rejection. She often remembered her mother's words, 'Don't expect to be liked but do make sure you are admired.'

During her student years she began to understand more clearly the sacrifices her mother and great-aunts had made to survive and achieve what they had, and the tough independence they needed. She really admired that, and visited one or two of the surviving relatives of that generation to talk to them about their lives. She had a book of their photographs and their letters, including one written from Holloway by Florence where she had been force-fed. She felt she was heir to a tradition, she was carrying on the torch.

When she thought about her father she always smiled. The few times she could remember in her childhood, of totally outrageous fun, had always been with her father, generally when they had sneaked off together. It was always a bit conspiratorial with him. He used to wink at her and pull funny faces behind the backs of the aunts when they were at their most serious. He was also the only one in the family she ever saw let go of his feelings – he would sometimes laugh uncontrollably, occasionally shout and lose his temper, and once he had broken down and cried unconsolably. Increasingly, this show of feelings had embarrassed Alison, as it clearly embarrassed her mother and other relatives, and much to her shame now she realised she had come to look down on him, as in truth he was not a very clever or indeed a very reliable man. He had worked on trade journals but had lost his job twice. When unemployed, and increasingly in his free time when employed, he spent his time out of the house in his allotment or with his mates at the legion club. Alison thought of him as a weak, unambitious man, but now she knew he was the one person she had truly and unconditionally loved, and his death when she was at college had devastated her.

She does not remember hearing many fairy tales and children's stories in her childhood, though reading and story-telling were major activities. She was passionately fond of the Arthurian tales, attracted to the leader who took over a disintegrating society and created a just, prosperous and peaceful kingdom. The stories of Hercules and Odysseus also attracted her, the heroes who tackled task after task to achieve their goal. But she was also fascinated by the stories of women explorers – Mary Kingsley, Freya Stark and others, and for a time at school her great heroine had been Clare Francis.

So, much of her life up to this point has been apparently successful and she still sees more peaks to conquer. She was nicknamed 'the professor' for a time when she was a child, and her ambition and intended plan is to become a university professor by the time she is 50. That will, she feels, complete her journey. As 'Professor Mapp' she will feel the approbation of all the relatives and teachers, both dead and alive, who have helped her on her journey. But though she seldom has time to dwell on things outside her work, when she does face those moments, she often feels that her life is flat and unsatisfactory. She still experiences strong emotions of being an outsider – always on the outside of a group or a party. She does not feel she is an attractive and loveable person to other people, and often wonders of her senior staff, 'Do they really like me?' If only she could relax more in social settings and just go and have fun and let her hair down. She really finds that very difficult. She certainly does experience moments of intense enjoyment but always in solitary moments, out walking on the hills or listening to and playing music.

Her relationships have not been long-lasting, though she has lived with her present partner for five years. There is something about giving herself to others, being totally intimate, sharing moments of fun and pain that she just finds difficult to do. All three of her partners have been open, fun-loving though generally gentle men, willing to support her in her work and live with her tendency of debating and discussing every issue that comes up.

Her present partner, Charles, has moved between jobs and does not seem to be making much of a career for himself, but has been a good support to her, and does try hard to help her relax and enjoy herself. The trouble is she is not sure she really wants to. She enjoys her work, being in charge, striding forward on her own. That is the easy part. The hard part is her life with other people. At least at work, however, she has found things rather easier since Frazer arrived. She appointed him because he shared many of her ideas about standards and college philosophy, and combined a gentle manner with strong and effective management. He really seems to be someone with whom she could work well.

Alison knows, as she reflects on these thoughts, that it may be time to start making some new decisions about herself. Maybe the second half of her life does not have to be the same as the first.

COMMENTARY

Alison's life and personality are of course infinitely richer than the above reflections would on their own indicate. Nevertheless, they do illuminate some of the key parts of her script. The concept of scripts is explained in chapter 9. It is enough to state here that it is a metaphor for the way in which during our early years we make major decisions about how our life is going to be, the broad paths we see it following, the beliefs that underlie that, and how we then set about making all this come true.

In Alison's script, an important element is that it is a winning rather than a losing script. This does not mean that it is without difficulties. There are sacrifices Alison has made, some self-destructive rather than enhancing decisions, and some serious limitations on the possibilities of personal growth, but it is basically a script for success in life. From her birth, all the influences around her were pressing her to seek and expect high achievement – in the stories round her birth, her name, the modelling of adults around her, and the reinforcing messages subsequently from her teachers. Although it was still her choice, it was always likely that she would see the life stretching in front of her as one of hard and rewarding work with an emphasis on cleverness and educational success. During her childhood, the use of her Adult ego state was actively encouraged, partly by the commitment to learning and solving problems, partly because so much of her time and conversation was spent with grown-ups. In fact her script did not give much emphasis to fun, and though she had much enjoyment and high spirits in her intellectual development, she missed out on much play with other children. Her Free Child state was in danger of atrophy.

She had a strong script message about being independent, self-reliant and confident in her own powers, as were the heroes of her childhood. Most of the time she is happy to take on life without expecting a supporting team to help her. She is not exactly a loner, because she needs other people to be in position while she tackles her work, but they are more like the props to her performance than equal actors.

Another script message was derived from her suffragette great-aunt and her mother. Everything she saw, and no doubt what she heard as well, would inform her that women take the responsible, dominant role, and that men will probably be unreliable and more inclined to fool about than take life on, as was the case with her father. Though she was well enough aware of sexist prejudice, as this was the small change of conversation in her childhood home, her own destiny to reach the top was wholly embraced by her. What she did get from her father was some compensatory Free Child activity. It was with him that she could get into trouble, make fun of her aunts behind their backs, and secretly have knock-about adventures. And though she admired her mother and loved her of course, the deep, unbounded love was for her father. There was a part of her that was at war, duplicating the underlying struggle between her mother and father. There was not much doubt which had been the winning side in her life so far, and she tended to transfer the script messages of that side to the way she treated the men in her professional life. She knew she was inclined to look down on them, assume they were not as strong or clever as herself, and she caught herself sometimes putting them down (in her mind if not in practice) with an acerbic word or withering look.

Another part of her script was that she was not destined to be popular, to be the centre of the group, socially active and in demand by others. Her self-image was strong, but she imagined others saw her in a negative way. She did not believe she was particularly attractive either in personality or appearance. She had always felt, and accepted, being a bit of an outsider, at school, university and in her various jobs, and this was just the way she believed life was for her.

At a deeper level there is a script message about intimacy. One of the important script permissions is that it is OK to be close to others, but Alison's message was nearer the script injunction 'don't be close'. This will certainly affect her behaviour at work. She may well set up games, the pay-off of which is to avoid getting too close to her colleagues, and she will be assisted by her Be Strong driver and her self-righteous racket.

Note that Alison, for all her enthusiasm for high standards, has not got a Be Perfect driver. Her commitment to excellence comes from her Adult ego state. She is in control, makes choices, moves her energy to where it can have maximum effect, and makes the best use of all her resources to achieve the most excellent results possible. That is quite different to her state when governed by her Be Strong driver. In that case she is not in control but under a compulsion to behave in certain ways so as to avoid acute discomfort. She cannot bear to be dependent on another. In her youth she greatly enjoyed playing her clarinet and winning at tennis, but could never have taken part in rock-climbing when her life depended on another's skill.

Her Be Strong driver comes not from her rational Adult but an archaic Child state. This distinction between behaviour under our Adult control and behaviour under our driver compulsion is very important to understand.

The script message, 'don't be close', has its most powerful impact in her personal relationships. The fear of intimacy combined with her subdued Free Child and her early decisions about where men seem to fit into the scheme of things, is likely to lead to a repetitive behaviour of failed relationships with pleasant but weak men. The relationship is likely to have problems over the level of intimacy each separately want, and she is likely to have the same ambivalent relationship with her partner as she had with her father – a reliance on this as a rare source of fun and relaxation, but uneasiness that it is a waste of her time. A supporting script injunction she has accepted is not to show her feelings, to keep control over her emotions. Though this has its uses at work, it has been devastating to the quality of her closest relationships.

Even at work her relationship with male colleagues may be problematic. She is drawn to men who are sympathetic and gentle, and in Frazer she has found someone who shares many of her beliefs, and unlike her father and partners, seems a bright and successful manager. She already shows signs of sharing moments of intimacy with him in a way she does not with any other. If this pairing becomes too obvious, it may well cause comment and resentment from other senior managers.

It was not inevitable that Alison made the decisions she did about what her life was going to be. Given the messages a child is receiving, often in an ambiguous or veiled way, it is sometimes remarkable the unusual way she may make sense of it all and envisage her future life. Nevertheless, the messages in Alison's case were strong and mutually reinforcing so it is unsurprising she made the decisions she did. An alternative for her would have been to decide, probably in her teens, that she was going to throw everything overboard and be the complete opposite of what everyone expected. She could, for example, have failed at school, dropped out of society, and become heavily dependent on her friends. This behaviour in TA terms is going into the anti-script. It is not a free choice but a reaction choice. She would have been as much a prisoner of her script having to do the opposite, as accepting the messages she had been given.

Alison, however, did not choose that path. Her choice now is to decide whether it is time to look at her present life and how she would like it to be in the future, and ask of each part of her script: accepting this was once useful to me, is it now useful? If it is not I will work to change it. So she takes a piece of paper to put down her thoughts and heads it:

Sylvia Alison Mapp.

Chapter 4

Mona's interview

By the summer term it was clear that Frazer would have to get down to conducting the formal staff development interviews.

These had been brought in under the old regime and staff and unions had steadfastly refused to accept the words 'appraisal' or 'individual performance review'. After much negotiation the title staff review interview was agreed, but even this name did not allay the fears of some staff.

'Thin end of the wedge,' was how some put it. 'Pay against performance' was another of the phrases. 'What performance? Exam results? What about the poor blighters teaching Meat 1?' All these questions, and more, were bandied around.

Nevertheless, it was in place and had to be done and Frazer felt a mixture of pleasure and trepidation at setting aside time to see each of his staff individually. He had attended a course on conducting such interviews and was meticulous in his preparation. He had a tray of tea and biscuits sent up and waited to meet Mona, his first interviewee, a lecturer in community care.

Have you ever experienced getting off on the wrong foot? Frazer couldn't believe what was happening. It had started well, or so he thought. He'd welcomed her and began the interview by asking her about herself and clarifying ideas before thinking to offer tea. This she refused crossly and seemed to become more and more upset and angry the more Frazer questioned her. He was utterly perplexed. Surely he was following procedure, surely she realised he wanted to know about her work and what she had done for the past year, what her plans were for the next, what had gone badly, what had gone well? He was new to the job after all.

Mona appeared more and more agitated and responded to his questions in monosyllables. He asked her eventually if she was upset about anything and then he got the lot. The years of neglect, her problems with Daphne, another colleague in the department, the amount of work she had to do, her worries about a particular student, the irritation with two of the placements which had been singularly unhelpful to her students, her lack of space, and a lot more besides. Frazer felt as if he had been swamped by a tidal wave and found himself backing off from this colleague. He found himself thinking, why doesn't she stop and think about each of these. There's bound to be a solution – one at a time please!

Mona felt that he wasn't interested in her problems. She resented him throwing everything back for her to work out. She wanted to be understood, for someone to show her kindness, sympathy, appreciation – I do so much for those girls, and that bloody Daphne, so high and mighty, is always finding fault and trying to take over. Wouldn't it be wonderful if just for once somebody said 'Well done Mona'? I hate this place – and many more thoughts besides.

The interview ground on with the tea drunk half stewed towards the end. Both were left with a feeling that no real contact had been made and that it was all a waste of time.

Later the same day Frazer conducted two more interviews and each followed an entirely different pattern. By the end of the week he was pretty certain with whom he felt comfortable and with whom he had to tread warily. Managing people was more of a minefield that one would expect.

COMMENTARY

The above scene illustrates the dynamics behind the Process communication model (see chapter 11 for an in-depth study). People are very different in their preferred modes of contact; some will only respond to a feeling overture. This could be a smile, an enquiry as to how they are feeling, some gesture that demonstrates contact at the level of emotions. Others would find this insulting and inappropriate and want to be contacted at the level of thinking, ideas and problem solving. They would feel uncomfortable at any feeling contact first. Yet others prefer to do something together first – play squash, go for a drink, get involved in the early stages of a project. They prefer initial contact to be at the level of behaviour. There are yet others who need a very gentle behavioural contact – the cup of tea, the walk around the department. Accepting that all people are unique, this model simply recognises some patterns that are observable in our preferences about how we are addressed, and how the process of the interaction continues.

The contact point, however, is only the beginning. It is about getting off on the right foot. After this initial contact an individual who wants, for example, to be met at a thinking level first, can then be approached at a feeling level. In the case of Mona, had she been contacted at a feeling level first, all Frazer's questions would have been answered with alacrity and clarity.

The encounter with Frazer also triggered off Mona's racket system. This is a self-perpetuating system that is triggered by a bad experience or feeling. It leads to an internal feedback loop which reinforces our negative beliefs about ourselves, our script decisions and various bodily postures and behaviours that are instantly recognisable to people who know us well. This system was devised by Richard Erskine and Marilyn Zalcman (1979). Mona's system would look something like **Figure 1.**

Figure 1: Mona's racket systems

Script belief	Rackety display
Belief about self I am unlovable, no one values or understands me	**Internal manifestation** Stomach ache, cramps in shoulders
Belief about others They are OK, they are sure of themselves	**External manifestation** Agitation, anger, stomping kind of walk
Quality of life It's not fair, no one listens to me, I hate it	**Fantasy** It doesn't matter how hard I try, it's no good

Thus Mona under stress appeared angry, unreasonable and volcanic, but although this was the feeling she experienced and expressed, it was in effect a substitute for her real emotions of sadness and hurt at not being understood and valued. Although there are many definitions of racket feelings which are listed in chapter 18, they are all in effect inauthentic feelings which buy into a person's frame of reference and act as a kind of self-fulfilling process which keeps the script alive.

Sometimes at work or in our personal lives we get locked in with people whose scripts in some way mesh with our own. It is then that we may experience interlocking racket systems. This was certainly true of Frazer and Mona. As a small boy Frazer had been very close to his mother, had picked up a lot of her mood changes and had tried to respond to them as best he could. But being a child, he did not have the resources to make things better. So over time, he found it safer to withdraw from any emotional scene and try to think rather than feel his way out of a difficult situation. At the end of his interview with Mona, he felt the same kind of frustration and anger he had felt as a child, helpless to reach the turbulent emotions of his mother. He resolved to have as little to do with Mona as possible. She went away with her script beliefs confirmed, that no one valued or understood her.

CHAPTER 5

A MELANGE OF MARKETING

A group of staff was meeting in the principal's office to discuss the corporate image of the college. They constituted the Marketing Committee and consisted of:

Les Brokenshaw, Marketing Co-ordinator and Chair of this committee;
Alison Mapp, Principal;
Steve Yates, Vice-Principal (Resources);
Carmella Amoroso, Head of Business Studies;
Michael Lee Grant, Community Liaison Officer and lecturer in social sciences; and
Nuala Toner, Deputy Head – School of Art.

Les allowed the meeting to drift into a discussion over a new college name to reflect the as yet undecided new corporate image.

Carmella was quite clear what the new name should be. 'I think we should call it Trentwood College.'

'Never,' said Steve. 'That makes it sound like some posh private school – nothing to do with the world of sweat and work, factories and offices.'

Les responded sharply, 'That isn't what we do anyway – at least we shouldn't be thinking of it. We are a college for all – responsive to the customers' needs.'

'I'm confused now,' replied Steve. 'If we are just a company out on the market getting customers and earning cash, then we might as well call ourselves Trentwood PLC.'

'I don't think that is what is meant,' said Michael. ('Yes it is,' *sotto voce* from Les).

'It means that we should be available for all the community. We are their college, we serve them, we belong to them. I think we should call ourselves Trentwood Community College.'

Steve intervened again. 'We've got to stick with Trentwood Technical College. That's what people are used to. They can remember that. We've always been a vocational college – starting with evening classes, building up day-release, then ONDs; we've a tradition and we shouldn't throw it away.'

Alison now joined in. 'That is just the point. We are not going to be like that in the future. We already are not, really. Over half our students are on general or recreational courses.'

'Then call yourself Trentwood Sixth Form College if that is what you want to be,' rejoined Steve, rather testily.

Nuala had tried to intervene two or three times and now made her point with some feeling. 'What I want you all to remember is that there is another college here as well, the Art College.'

'It's not a college any longer, Nuala, just a department,' interjected Carmella.

Ignoring the interruption, Nuala went on, 'Whatever name we have, we are not going to lose our name completely. We have a separate identity, a national reputation and we want to keep that.'

Isn't it odd, thought Alison, how we spend so much time and emotion whenever names come up, when there are really important things waiting to be done.

Actually it is not odd at all. What is going on here is no different from the discussions in families about an expected baby's name.

Naming has always been a very powerful action. It sets up expectations for the new child to live up to. It might be named after its mother or father, a famous person, a rich uncle, or it might be given a romantic name or the plainest name possible. In the same way, colleges are named to create expectations, to define how they should be, and if they want to change then renaming is a key part of that process. Chapter 9 on scripts describes how naming becomes part of the script of the child, and in the same way we can think of the organisation having its name within its script.

As the meeting progresses, members focus their thoughts more and more on the future of the college and the kind of corporate image they want to project. All have their own thoughts about the kind of place it is and should be.

Les had spent some minutes explaining the way in which the college could develop work outside its customary areas by moving into new market segments. Michael occasionally added one or two points in support, and Steve kept on prompting Les with sympathetic questioning. Steve then turned to Carmella with a slight smile on his face and said: 'How do you feel about this, Carm? You've done a bit of work in selling short courses, haven't you?'

'More than a bit,' responded Carmella tartly. 'We made a lot of money for the college last year and lots more to come. You can't hang about. You have to keep ahead of the game.'

'Yes, that does seem to have been forgotten, doesn't it Les?' said Steve. Les' response, which was to explain how the college had to move on from the usual full-cost short courses to a more imaginative use of all the college's resources in the market, began to irritate Carmella who felt her work was being denigrated. A couple more interjections from Steve kept the issue developing and her anger flared up. Les responded in kind, though not with quite such vehemence. Steve turned to the principal with a look of pained forebearance, his eyes eloquently saying: how can we get on when these two are quarrelling like this?

Subsequently Carmella regretted her outburst, which earned a rebuke from the principal, and driving home that evening she ruefully thought how often she ended up losing her temper. It had always been the same since she was a child. Her father, mother, aunts and brothers were all short-tempered. All she could remember from her childhood were constant rows or people rushing off after abrupt put-downs. If you didn't stand up for yourself you didn't get anywhere, and if you tried to be reasonable or defuse a row, people just didn't have the time and walked away. She did not really have bad feelings towards the people she rowed with. She just seemed to get sucked into these outbursts. Afterwards she always regretted it. At this point in her musing, she broke off to loudly curse a driver who jumped in front of her and then dropped speed so she had to slow down.

What is going on here? Carmella has been a victim at the meeting of a manipulation which in TA terms is called a game. Games are analysed and described in chapter 12, but the above is a good illustration. Steve has set up Les and Carmella to fight and then sat back to enjoy the spectacle. He has done it under the guise of being reasonable, but his interventions had all been aimed at getting Carmella to respond to Les. He knows that she has a short fuse, and that Les is not slow to respond if he is attacked, so setting up the game in any meeting is pretty straightforward. Though games are destructive, and certainly this episode did nothing to help the meeting forward, the people involved take part because they get something out of it. Until Carmella confronts this in herself, she will remain an easy prey to be hooked into the game.

Michael was explaining how the college had very little real understanding of the various ethnic groups in the community.

'All most of you know is that there is a large black population, and that Afro-Carribbeans outnumber Asians. You are all well-intentioned but also ignorant.'

Alison intervened at this point. 'That's all very well, Michael, and probably true, but it is your job to make sure we have this information. We need it quickly, so I want you to give us a full report at the next meeting with full facts and figures about the main groups out there.'

'Well, I don't know about that. It's a complicated business, and I have got a heavy teaching load just at the moment.'

'Come on, Michael,' replied Alison. 'You raised the issue. It is clearly important and we want the figures you have got. It is three weeks before the next meeting. That should be time enough, shouldn't it?'

'I don't know. I really need six weeks at least.'

'Three weeks, Michael.'

'Well, OK, I'll try my best.'

'Without fail, Michael. We want to be on our way. We cannot afford to hang about.'

Michael has been set up for another game. He has taken on a task that he knows he cannot achieve in time. When he fails to have the report ready at the next meeting, the principal will publicly rebuke him and make him feel a failure with that self-righteous tone she sometimes adopts. He will get psychologically kicked, and have reinforced the feeling he often has of life being unfair and his efforts always fouling up. Alison, on the other hand, needs to feel on top of her job every so often by being able to publicly rebuke one of her staff. It is a need she has had for many years. Even at school, she felt the need sometimes to be in the right and criticise the other pupils. She did it at home as well to her partner – just like her grandmother used to do to everyone.

So both Alison and Michael are satisfying the needs of a negative bit of their character. Organisations give them plenty of scope to do this. Of course, if they did not want to play games, they could instead work out a sensible strategy for collecting the information the meeting needs, but really neither is at that moment interested in that. They both collude to set up a task they know will end in failure.

To Steve, who is the longest-serving member of staff present, the college is still really Bob Bingley's place. Bingley had become principal in 1946 when the college was very small. Nearly all the students and staff were part-time. Most of the students were day-release and evening attenders from local industry. Bob Bingley was a blunt, no-nonsense, larger than life character who transformed the college over the next 35 years, building up new courses, departments, buildings, and staff. The college throughout this time retained the sub-culture of the engineering world from which Bob had come, and which accounted for the largest number of students. Bob was an autocrat. He did not believe much in consultation, and ran the college from his office in his way. He had a lot of personal friends among the factory owners in the area, and it was through his network of relationships outside the college that he kept the students flowing in and the buildings going up. There were many stories still circulating among the older staff of his rough humour and abrupt manner with anyone he did not like. He did not believe in frills, and this included many of the things he dismissed as 'trendy' that were becoming common in the '70s – student counsellors, equal opportunities, special needs, life and social skills. Though he seized the opportunity to expand into GCEs, social work and other similar courses, he was still at heart wedded to the education of apprentices in the manufacturing industry, and to City and Guilds and National Certificates and Diplomas. Steve had been his protégé, and was deeply attached to that kind of college.

Alison, however, saw a college that was stuck in the past, which had put too little energy into recent curriculum initiatives, and which had traditional and rather mediocre standards of student achievement and teacher performance. This was reflected in the indifference to the appearance of the grounds and buildings, the macho image of many of the workshops and teaching rooms, and the traditional style of departmental organisation. In many ways it was an anti-intellectual place. This had begun to change a little under her immediate predecessor, but there had been no real drive for high standards and quality provision. She was determined to create the best college in the region, and by that she meant the one that achieved the best student results and had the best reputation as a high-flying college. To do that she put great store on two things; the improvement of teaching and tutoring skills of the staff, and a physical environment that attracted students and the public alike.

Michael saw a different kind of college for the future. His parents had come to the Midlands from Barbados in the late 1950s, and he had been born and brought up locally. He knew the other people sitting there simply could not understand the experience of being a black child at school, a black student at polytechnic, and a black teacher in the college. All his life he had faced minor and sometimes major discrimination. Though he was not comfortable with his role as the black teacher responsible for multi-cultural and racial issues, he was passionately committed to the concept of a community college which provided for those in the locality already educationally disadvantaged, for whom most colleges, including this one, did little or nothing. He wanted the college of the future to be a microcosm of the community, attracting not simply the minority ethnic groups and those with special needs, but all those who had lost out in the process of previous institutional education. He imagined a college that would be very open, with flexible learning programmes set up for the convenience of the learner, not the staff, and with an informal culture of sub-groups freely expressed in festivals, concerts and other happenings. For this to develop he knew that those with power, such as the principal and senior managers and also the lecturers in the classroom, would have to give much up and allow those in the community themselves to make decisions. His most frequent statement was: 'we must return the college to the people'. He thought it was unlikely it would happen though he would fight for it. He saw the college wedded to its own prejudices and its own comfort. It had successfully erected barriers that prevented the use of its facilities by most of the community in order that it could carry on doing what it had always done for a small minority.

Les was clear that the world of the past was over. The college had been publicly and fairly generously supported to provide vocational training in a number of traditional and now declining areas, and had never had to worry about competition. The money arrived each year irrespective of how well the college was performing , and in some areas the quality had been poor. Many employers, particularly outside the traditional engineering field, had become unenthusiastic about the college's capacity to respond to their training needs. He had no doubt they should now seize the opportunity given by changes in the governance and funding of colleges, to get rid of the dead hand of the LEA and work with the TECs, market themselves vigorously and be ultra-responsive to changes in demand. Unless they went whole-heartedly for this then he had little doubt the college would close down in three or four years. The future lay with the sharp, smart outfit, quick on its feet and with a strong public profile.

These four members are all looking for ways to understand how the college has been, what it could become and what might prevent that. There are various frameworks that might help them in their thinking. TA offers the metaphor of the organisational script. This is described in detail in chapter 10, but we can see that just by considering the points made by the four committee members, this college has been living out a script that was written for it in its first few years. In the script there is a dominant founder figure who shaped the college in its growing years. The college staff learned what was acceptable and what was not. Those who stayed accepted the script of the organisation, whose vision was local not regional or national, industrial rather than commercial or general, and male rather than female. It was a relatively unambitious script, which looked sceptically at new developments and believed in conservative steady growth in a world it knew. It eschewed risk-taking or adventure. In some ways it was a script that limited intellectual developments. It did not ask too much of people – just that they did their job conscientiously and did not make trouble. It was a script that asked for average performance, but nothing special. There was no excitement to produce top quality work for a top quality college. The metaphor of the script as applied to the college is an extension of its application to the individual and the development of his or her life; and as with the individual the organisation can reach points when it is appropriate to decide whether current script messages are still relevant. This was what the members of the marketing committee are doing.

INTRODUCTION TO THE SECOND
PART OF THE BOOK

In the first section of the book, we have introduced most of the concepts of transactional analysis in the process of looking at some of the events at Trentwood College. These have included:
- ego states;
- strokes;
- scripts;
- organisational scripts;
- process communication;
- games;
- time structuring;
- drivers; and
- rackets.

In the second section of the book, a chapter is devoted to each of the TA concepts. These can either be read on their own or used as support chapters to the points raised in the discussion of events at Trentwood College.

CHAPTER 6
EGO STATES

Ego states are the central building blocks of transactional analysis and a way of putting names to experiences with which we are all familiar – namely that there are times when we feel very much in the present and in touch with what our environment has to offer us, times when we feel as we did at some time in our past, and other occasions when we find ourselves behaving like a person we knew from our past.

Paul Federn first described these phenomena as states of the ego, which Eric Berne, the founder of transactional analysis, changed to 'ego states'.

In order to understand the richness of transactional analysis, it is necessary to begin by understanding the 'structural model'.

THE STRUCTURAL MODEL

The structural model is a way of describing the makeup of a personality. It can also be used to describe a team, group or organisation, and this will be considered at the end of this chapter. However, its primary use has been to address the multitudinous elements of the human personality.

The three ego states which are described by the structural model are:
- the Archaic or Historical Child ego state;
- the Integrated Adult ego state;
- the Introjected Parent ego state.

The first and third belong to another time or place. Only the integrated adult is concerned with current reality.

At their simplest, they are traditionally drawn as shown in **Figure 2**.

The model can be understood by taking each ego state in turn, elaborating it, and giving examples drawn from life.

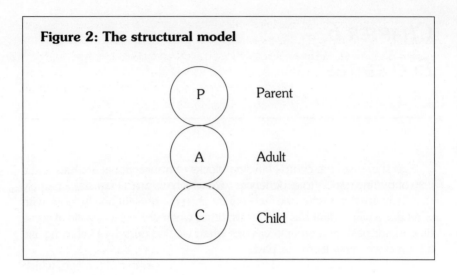

Figure 2: The structural model

P   Parent

A   Adult

C   Child

The Child ego state

The Child ego state is the complex history that each of us brings to any given situation. It includes our national temperament and rhythms, our early experiences, traumata, the ways we have of adapting to our family, school and the world in which we find ourselves.

In some ways it is reminiscent of the annual rings of a tree with different development stages in our lives being apparent: some showing years of plenty, some drought (deficit), hiccups in our growth (lesions) and influences from outside (see **Figure 3**).

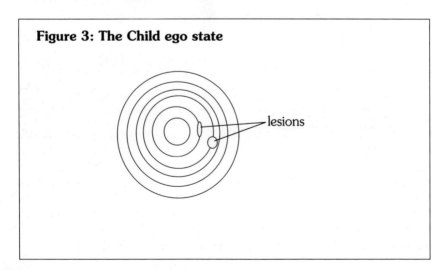

Figure 3: The Child ego state

lesions

The Child ego state contains our natural selves and the overlays and adaptations we have had to make in order to survive. Thus each Child is unique and special. **Figure 3** is the model favoured by Bernd Schmidt (1990) and, in slightly different form, by Fanita English (1977). The more common representation of the Child ego state is called the Second Order Structural Model and is used by Berne (1975) and others (see **Figure 4**).

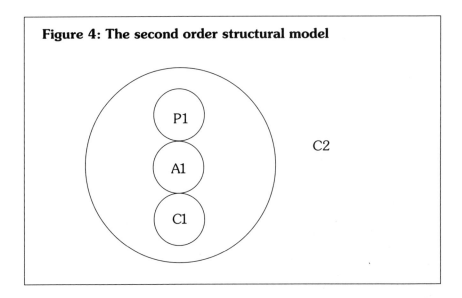

Figure 4: The second order structural model

The C1, also known as the Somatic Child, is the part of ourselves that has very early developmental origins that took in the world through physical contact and through the senses. Thus a baby who was not fed when it was hungry, nor changed and warmed when it was wet and cold, may become oblivious to its bodily needs and in time become unaware of the need to eat, sleep or feel the changes in the weather. One example of this was a man who regularly forgot to eat for 12 hours at a time and who regularly came to visit in the winter wearing a short-sleeved shirt, no jacket, no scarf and no gloves.

The A1 is charmingly referred to by Berne as the Little Professor. It is indicative of the developing intelligence of the child and is characterised by an intuitive assessment of what is going on out there in the big wide world. When people use the term 'sussing out a situation' what they may be accessing is their little professor. An example of this might be an acute awareness of a hidden agenda at a meeting – the covert business.

The P1 is known by a variety of names, the most useful being the Magical Parent – a term coined by Ian Stewart (Stewart and Joines 1987) which relates to the growing child's incorporation of aspects of significant parental figures in the environment which, due to the child's limited power of understanding, become imbued with powers that seem almost magical. So, for example, when a child sees an overtired or anxious parent acting in a cross or irrational way, she may assume that this parent is angry with her for, for example, hitting a classmate at school that day.

In the face of such complexity in our childhood environment, the Archaic Child in each of us made a series of decisions about ourselves and how to act, think and feel in certain situations. These decisions helped us to adapt to our environment then, but may have no place in the current structure of the here and now.

Thus, in any situation, such as visiting our children's school or on parents' evening, or taking a job at a new college, we will be bringing to it our own history of previous experiences, some good, some painful, that may be activated, either consciously or unconsciously, if something or somebody triggers a painful memory for us.

The Parent ego state

In addition to our Child ego state we also carry another historical part of ourselves into any encounter. This is the Parent ego state and is a collection of significant figures (teachers, older siblings, parents and heroes or heroines from books, films or television) that we have in some sense swallowed whole. These are called introjections. They accompany us into many aspects of our lives, though we are often unaware of their presence, and they affect our responses to cultural norms, our manners and the ways we have of doing things. Each family has its own preferred way of doing things: preparing food, celebrating festivals and even washing themselves. Within the Parent ego state reside cultural norms and values, belief systems and prejudices. One way of reaching these internalised messages is to think about the proverbs and sayings which we have internalised. Sometimes, because they are often activated without our awareness, we can be affronted by the behaviour of some people without really knowing why. It is for this reason that some of the best relationships are between people who share the same basic core values.

The Parent ego state in structural analysis second order diagrams is shown in **Figure 5**.

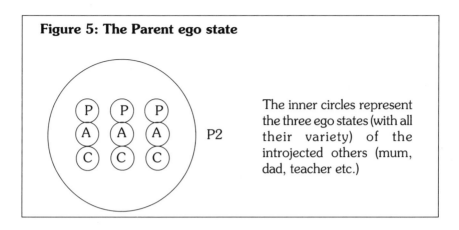

Figure 5: The Parent ego state

The inner circles represent the three ego states (with all their variety) of the introjected others (mum, dad, teacher etc.)

The Adult ego state

Finally we come to the Integrated Adult ego state, which belongs to the present. It is comprised of what Berne called feelings, attitudes and behaviours, which relate directly to the environment as it now presents itself. Rather than attitudes, it may be more accurate to use 'thoughts', because any attitude is itself made up of the three elements – feelings, thoughts and behaviour. **Figure 6** shows the Integrated Adult ego state.

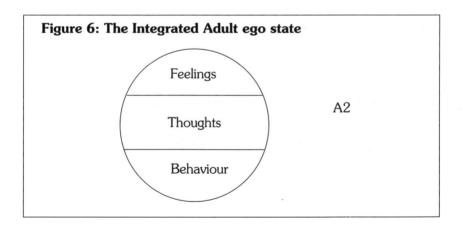

Figure 6: The Integrated Adult ego state

It is, therefore, clear from a transactional analysis viewpoint, that any of us walking into any given situation will take all three ego states with us (see **Figure 7**). What is not clear, however, is which ego state is being activated!

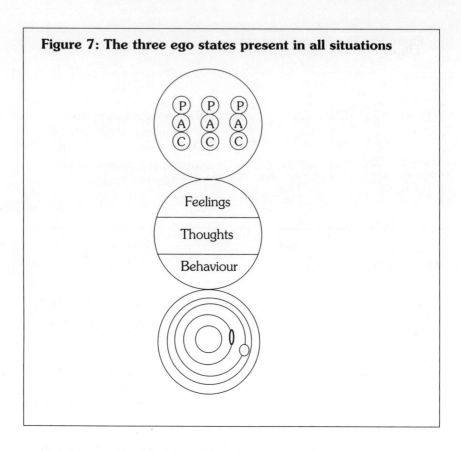

Figure 7: The three ego states present in all situations

This brings us to the outward manifestations of these ego states.

THE FUNCTIONAL MODEL: EXPRESSIONS OF BEHAVIOUR

The way we get clues as to what ego state a person is coming from is through their actions, and for this reason Berne developed the 'functional model of ego states'. Though composed of the similar three circles, the circles here refer to outer demonstrations (behaviour), which relate to the hidden and often unknown parts of the personality discussed in the section above on the structural model. **Figure 8** shows the functional model in its most simple form.

The Functional Parent is divided into the Nurturing Parent and the Controlling Parent. Nurturing Parent behaviours are the acts of kindness, care, consideration, protectiveness and general care-taking that we can all manifest at some time. How we do this will depend on our role models and our experiences in our own lives.

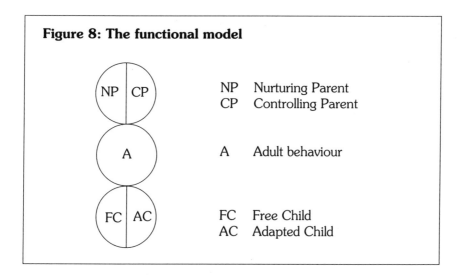

Figure 8: The functional model

NP	Nurturing Parent
CP	Controlling Parent
A	Adult behaviour
FC	Free Child
AC	Adapted Child

Controlling Parent behaviours are rule-making, creating boundaries, punishing and criticising. These too will come from our own repertoire gleaned from Introjected Parent figures and childhood experiences.

Adult behaviour, in terms of functional analysis, refers to thinking, quantifying, investigating and asking for more information. Functional Adult behaviour is characterised by questions and phrases such as when, how often, give me an example, and what is the outcome. It is behaviour best described as investigative.

The Functional Child is divided into the Free Child (or Natural Child) and the Adapted Child. Our spontaneous awareness of joy, feelings, sensations and stimuli and our responses to them are the behavioural manifestations of the Free Child ego state. The Adapted Child includes the range of behaviours which we call on from our vast repertoire of responses shaped to the demands of the adults in our lives when we were children. Some of these are very useful and can be used appropriately in novel situations, but some of them will be situation-specific, historically speaking, and are no longer either desirable or appropriate responses to any current situation.

The following situation demonstrates how structural ego state experience informs functional behaviour. I had been sitting with two male colleagues who were enjoying a fascinating conversation on an area of interest they shared and about which I knew very little. I listened with interest. However, later two more colleagues arrived and my Parent introject, which is concerned with beliefs about courtesy over introductions, was activated. No introductions were made and I found myself visiting an Archaic Child place of not being quite sure what to do in the situation. Metaphorically, I hopped from foot to foot, wondering when someone would introduce the newcomers. In the end

53

I introduced myself, feeling taken aback and rather uncomfortable because the here and now did not fit with either my normal historical experience or my beliefs about how to take care of people. Reflecting on the situation, it is clear that my behavioural mode was to withdraw. This is an example of a structural contamination (**Figure 9**), with Parental values being activated and Child feelings of not mattering surfacing.

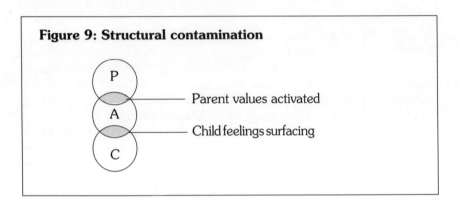

Figure 9: Structural contamination

— Parent values activated

— Child feelings surfacing

In behavioural terms I could have gone into a Controlling Parent mode and demonstrated my sense of affront or I could have used any of the other functional forms of behaviour. What I chose to do was a mixture of Adult assessment of the situation and Adapted Child which was to remove myself from conflict.

It is possible to further divide the functional model (i.e. expressions of behaviour) in the Parent and Child ego states into positive and negative aspects (see **Figure 10**).

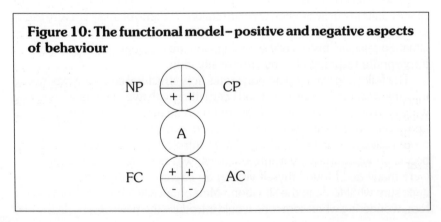

Figure 10: The functional model – positive and negative aspects of behaviour

Positive nurturing is sympathetic to the here and now: it is environmentally sensitive and appropriate. Over-nurturing, or rescuing, is negative and is manifested by smothering, inappropriate touch and doing things for others which they can and want to do for themselves. It is a way of controlling others.

Similarly, the Controlling Parent, in its positive form, shows clear boundary setting and constructive, critical feedback, whereas the negative Controlling Parent is destructive, gratuitously critical and harshly judgemental.

Within the Child ego state the positive Free Child is the fun, laughter, tears, awareness of fatigue, body rhythms, fear, anger and sadness which are honest and authentic expressions of feelings that are in tune with the environment and the person. The negative Free Child state occurs in situations that call for measured behaviour so it is concerned with the inappropriateness of expressions of immediate feelings, for example, running about in the middle of an important meeting!

Positive Adapted Child responses are typified by the kinds of behaviour that we teach our children and that we ourselves were taught in order to live at peace with our fellow beings, for example, table manners and modes of dress. Negative Adapted Child behaviour is dysfunctional in the here and now, but which had currency in our families of origin, for example, over-politeness and over-self depreciation.

When people are operating from an uncontaminated Integrated Adult, they might choose to exhibit positive Controlling Parent, positive Nurturing Parent, positive Adapted Child, positive Free Child or positive Adult behaviours, in all their many forms, depending upon the situation. Contaminations are likely to produce negative Controlling Parent, negative Nurturing Parent, negative Adapted Child, and negative Free Child behaviours.

Figure 11 shows how the structural and the functional models can work together.

Ego states can be diagnosed behaviourally, socially, historically and phenomenologically. Behavioural manifestations have already been discussed – i.e. that the energy invested in different ego states manifests in different outward behaviours. Sometimes an inner Archaic Child might manifest as external Controlling Parent behaviour. Social diagnosis occurs when we find ourselves responding to someone as though they were a child or a parent figure. These two forms of diagnosis tend to be reflected most clearly in the functional model. Historical diagnosis occurs when we find ourselves behaving, for example, like we did when we were seven years old at the start of the new school term.

Phenomenological indicators relate to the inner feeling of being that seven year old – the stomach churning, the fight/flight reactions and shyness.

Figure 11: The influence of the structural model on the functional model

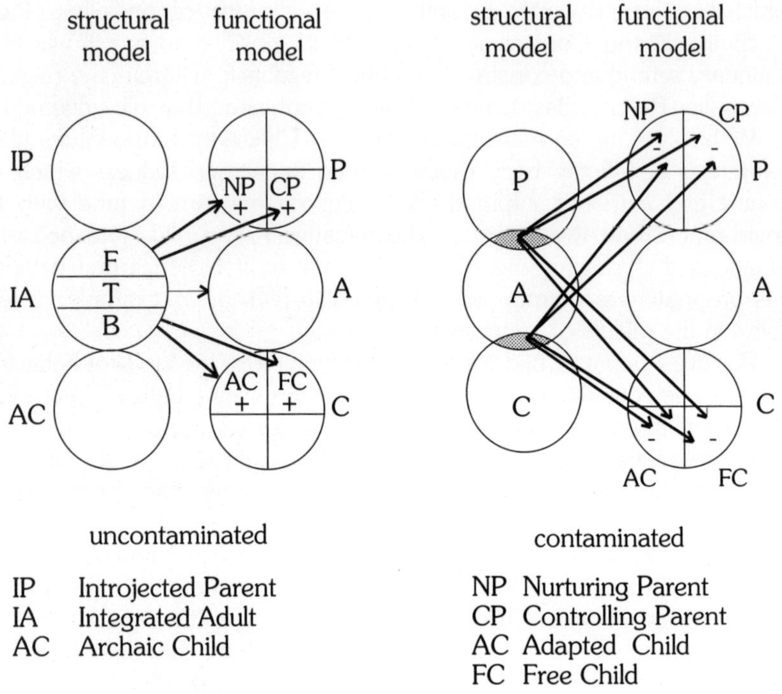
structural model
functional model
structural model
functional model
IP
P
NP
CP
+
+
F
IA
T
A
B
AC
FC
+
+
AC
C
P
NP
CP
P
A
A
C
C
AC
FC
uncontaminated
contaminated
IP Introjected Parent
IA Integrated Adult
AC Archaic Child
NP Nurturing Parent
CP Controlling Parent
AC Adapted Child
FC Free Child

ORGANISATIONAL APPLICATION

Ego states are very useful in developing a sense of organisational structure. Some institutions and bodies are very parental in their ethos. Senior management teams are seen to make decisions with little or no consultation with other colleagues and pass them down the line to 'the children' working further down the hierarchy. An ego state portrait of such an organisation could look something like **Figure 12.**

Other types of organisation, such as theatre companies, might appear to have more Child energy available and look something like **Figure 13**.

Conversely a firm of accountants, for example, might appear to be weighted in favour of the Adult side with a strong dose of Parent (**Figure 14**).

How we experience our organisation can affect how we behave within it. It is often acknowledged that capable adults behave like cowed children in the face of some autocratic institutions. Too much paternalism, for that matter, can engender rebellious behaviour which is sometimes characterised by very strong union activity.

Figure 12: A Parental type of organisation	**Figure 13: A Child type of organisation**
	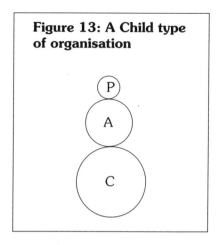

Figure 14: A strongly Adult organisation

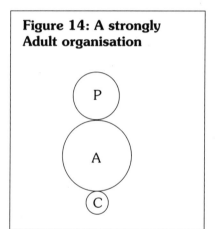

Figure 15: A well balanced organisation

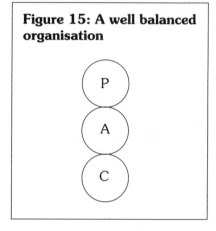

In colleges where management is seen as servicing the institution and responding to requests, a dialogue both up and down the line management structure is more likely to evoke Integrated Adult responses from both managers and other colleagues **(Figure 15)**. These workplaces listen, problem-solve, reward good ideas, take care of their employees as well as their clients, customers and students, and are characterised by higher levels of motivation and creativity than many places most of us have experienced in our working lives.

Part of the key to this is to keep Adair's (1984) three areas of responsibility well in focus **(Figure 16)**.

If one of the areas of responsibility demands too much energy at the expense of the others, the kind of ego state portraits drawn above may well be the outcome.

ANALYSIS OF TRANSACTIONS

Transactional analysis takes its name from the analysis of how people communicate. A person coming from Parent might be directing his or her message to someone else's Child (see **Figure 17**).

However, the receiver does have a choice as to whether he or she responds from the invited ego state. Steve Karpman highlights this notion of choice in his article entitled Options (1971). To begin with, it may seem difficult not to respond as an angry or frightened Child to a Controlling Parent transaction, but once we know that we can move in and out of ego states at our will, it enables us to increase our range and become more self-determining individuals.

Figure 18 illustrates a crossed transaction, where a Controlling Parent addresses an Adapted Child, but the response comes back from the Adult. The resulting outcome is a momentary pause in the dialogue as it was not the response the first speaker was expecting.

Another common experience is to hear a message stated on a social level, for example, 'Do come to dinner sometime', with an intuitive awareness that it means 'Whatever you do, don't take me up on that' (see **Figure 19**). These

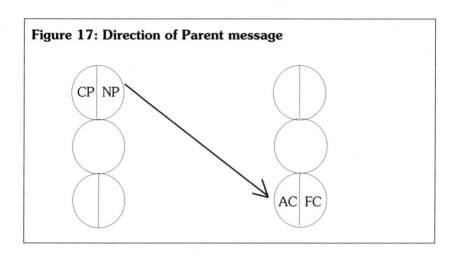

Figure 17: Direction of Parent message

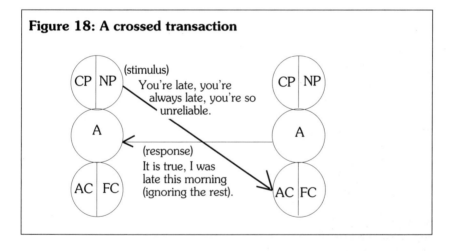

Figure 18: A crossed transaction

(stimulus)
You're late, you're always late, you're so unreliable.

(response)
It is true, I was late this morning (ignoring the rest).

are known as ulterior transactions and the outcome is usually determined at the psychological (i.e. ulterior) level. The recipient never gets asked for a specific dinner engagement and never forces the issue. Much humour is based on situations when the ulterior is ignored and the person responds to the social (overt) message – 'Yes, great, let's get our diaries out and see when we're both free.'

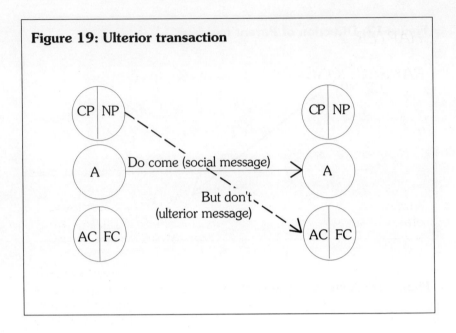

Figure 19: Ulterior transaction

CONCLUSION

Awareness of the concept of ego states can help us unravel tangles at work, at home and in other relationships. It can help us understand the elements of ourselves we bring into any situation and why some encounters hurt and others are so rewarding. It can also remind each of us that we carry around a sensitive child in our grown-up bodies that can react quite unexpectedly in some situations, and that some of the people in our past still have a voice today.

CHAPTER 7
TRANSACTIONS

The analysis of how people transact with one another is what gives transactional analysis its name.

A transaction is an exchange of strokes between two persons consisting of a stimulus and a response between specific ego states. A conversation is a series of transactions linked together. (Woollams and Brown, 1978)

In any interpersonal encounter there are a number of options open to us (Karpman, 1971). We can transact from a functional Adult ego state by asking for information, exchanging hypotheses or looking at the facts; from our Parent ego state by sharing our value systems and beliefs; and from our functional Child ego state by being enthusiastic, creative, curious or fun.

The range of potential behaviours from each ego state is far more extensive than the transactions given above which serve as examples only.

One of the crucial factors determining on what basis the conversation will continue, is the response of the other person to how we have just said what we have just said, e.g. 'I don't understand a word of this.'

'I'll read it again slowly and then you'll see what I mean.'

A complementary transaction is one where the stimulus and response vectors are parallel so that only two ego states are involved. More specifically, for a transaction to be complementary, it must fulfil two criteria:
- the response comes from the ego state to which it was directed; and
- the response is directed back to the ego state which first initiated the transaction.

This can be illustrated in **Figure 20**.

The first rule of communication is that, given complementary transactions, communication may continue indefinitely (until a crossed transaction occurs).

A crossed transaction occurs when the above criteria are not met, e.g. a person sends a request to another's Adult ego state and gets a response from that person's Controlling Parent (see **Figure 21**). Thus the ego state to which the communication was addressed is not the one which responds.

When this occurs the second rule of communication comes into operation – when a transaction is crossed, a breakdown (sometimes only brief) in communication results and something different is likely to follow.

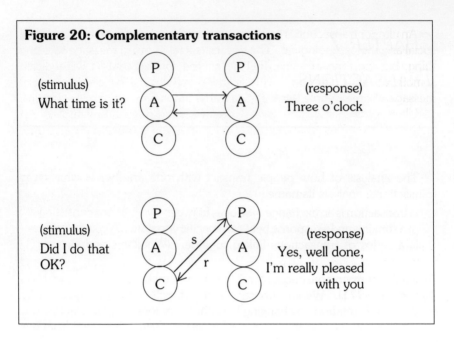

Figure 20: Complementary transactions

(stimulus)
What time is it?

(response)
Three o'clock

(stimulus)
Did I do that
OK?

(response)
Yes, well done,
I'm really pleased
with you

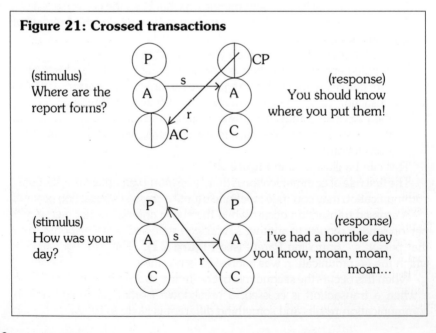

Figure 21: Crossed transactions

(stimulus)
Where are the
report forms?

(response)
You should know
where you put them!

(stimulus)
How was your
day?

(response)
I've had a horrible day
you know, moan, moan,
moan...

An ulterior transaction is a communication that operates on two levels; the social and the psychological. The surface (social or overt) message says one thing, but the tone of voice, that left unsaid, or the context will indicate something quite different. This is the psychological or ulterior (covert) message. Some people think that all transactions have an ulterior element.

Ulterior transactions are divided into two types, angular and duplex. An angular one involves three ego states, a duplex involves four (see **Figure 22**).

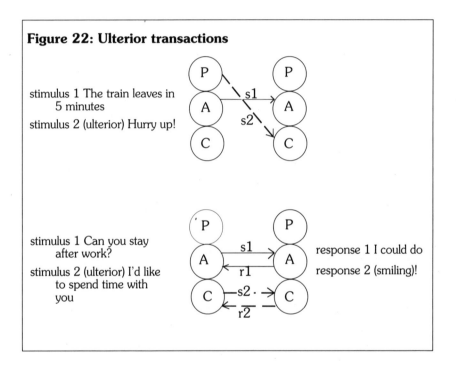

Figure 22: Ulterior transactions

stimulus 1 The train leaves in 5 minutes

stimulus 2 (ulterior) Hurry up!

stimulus 1 Can you stay after work?

stimulus 2 (ulterior) I'd like to spend time with you

response 1 I could do

response 2 (smiling)!

In the analysis of ulterior transactions we find a third rule of communication; namely that the outcome of the transaction will be determined on the psychological level rather than on the social level. That is why we have the expression 'coming away from an encounter with a bad taste in the mouth', or conversely, feeling wonderfully uplifted by something seemingly simply said.

In Broken Record – a technique of repeating a particular request or statement of intent over and over again and avoiding side traps – the person using this technique stays in his/her Adult ego state, avoiding any hooks inviting a response from the Nurturing Parent, Controlling Parent or any of the Child ego states. For example:

'Hi, Madeleine, do you fancy going to the staff disco?'

'No, I'm not going. Thanks for asking.'

'Oh come on, stop being a spoil sport,' (trying to hook into her Adapted Child).

'No, I'm not going,' (staying in Adult).

'Look, I really would appreciate you coming with me. I just never go out now, not since Doreen died,' (trying to hook her Nurturing Parent).

'I'm sorry you have no one to go with, but I am not going,' (staying in Adult).

'I know you've been working very hard and long hours recently. You deserve to have some fun just one evening,' (trying to hook her Free Child).

'I hope you have a really good time, but I am not going,' (staying in Adult).

Another example could be as follows:

'I need to have some papers printed for the conference next Tuesday.'

'No chance. You've brought them in far too late,' (trying to hook the Adapted Child).

'I realise it is a rush job, but it is a priority. I need to have them for next Tuesday,' (staying in Adult).

'How do you expect me to do that? It's the third priority job I've been given this morning, my assistant is off sick, I'm struggling with a cold. It's an impossible job this, and no one appreciates what I do,' (trying to hook the Nurturing Parent or, perhaps, Controlling Parent).

I do understand your difficulties and I will co-operate with you in any way we can negotiate, but I must have the papers for next Tuesday,' (staying in Adult).

'That's typical, isn't it? You people don't give one inch whatever problems the rest of us have,' (trying to hook into either Adapted Child or Controlling Parent).

'I know it must seem like that to you sometimes, but I must have the papers for Tuesday. Is there anything I can do to facilitate this?' (staying in Adult).

CHAPTER 8

STROKES

A stroke is any unit of attention given to the individual. Strokes are essential for the physical and psychological survival of every human being. From its earliest moments the newborn baby needs the experience of contact with other humans, and though the initial contact is likely to be mostly physical, as the baby grows into the young infant, child, adolescent; and adult so it will experience attention from others through speech and actions.

There is a minimal level of necessary stroking below which the child may not survive. It pines away with a malady known to Victorians as marasmus or withering. Above that minimal level many children may still have a serious deficiency of strokes that leaves them struggling for healthy psychological development. It is difficult to over-emphasise the importance of our early experience of stroking. In our search to understand ourselves as adults, it is a key that unlocks understanding of our patterns of behaviour and the legacy of our childhood that we choose to carry.

The following section categorises strokes in a number of different ways. The implications of those divisions will be analysed in the final section of the chapter.

LEVELS OF INTENSITY

A stroke can be no more than a nod from someone as they pass us in the corridor. It is not much of an expression of interest, but it is certainly qualitatively different from not being noticed at all. Strokes can range in intensity from that simple nod to the experience of someone noticing us, rushing towards us with open arms, saying, 'I've missed you so much while you've been away'. The strokes we receive are a mixture of strong and mild intensities, and to experience nothing but highly-charged strokes may be as uncomfortable as only receiving light strokes. We need to check that the mix of intensity that we experience seems healthy for us.

FREQUENCY

Some people throughout their life receive large numbers of strokes, while other people always seems to be on a meagre diet.

Commonly we may go through periods when our stroke diet becomes temporarily restricted, or when strokes in a particular area of our lives are hard to come by. It may feel as though we are on a desert island desperately looking for a footprint in the sand. This may be because of a move to a new job or department, or moving house; or it could be the result of sickness or old age. Some situations, relationships and organisations are stroke-rich, others are stroke-starved. We need to check if the number of strokes we receive in the various parts of our life is sufficient.

FORMS OF EXPRESSION

We can experience strokes through the spoken word or through written messages. We can experience strokes through physical touching, by handshakes or embraces. We can be stroked by the deeds people do for us that express their feelings towards us, by making us a cup of tea or taking us out on a trip. No one of these is better than the others, but at different times in their lives people do seem to have preferences both for the way they give and the way they receive strokes. It may be, however, that their fear of some expression of stroking, or their inability to notice one kind of stroke, has become limiting to their relationships and personal growth.

POSITIVE AND NEGATIVE STROKES

Up to this point we have assumed strokes are positive expressions of regard. Strokes, however, are simply units of attention of any kind given to another person. They can be pleasant, appreciative, supportive, and loving (positive), or unpleasant, critical, destructive, and hating (negative). Either way they are important because they acknowledge the fact that we exist. Beyond that critical base point however, there is clearly a world of difference in experiencing positive appreciation and negative put-downs. Claude Steiner caught the essence of this in his distinction between strokes by calling them warm fuzzies and cold pricklies. A negative stroke is certainly better than no stroke at all, and the child who is universally ignored will seek notice and painful recognition by misbehaviour. If you cannot get a kiss, then a cuff is better than nothing. The relative mix of positive and negative strokes we give and receive is an important piece of self-understanding.

CONDITIONAL AND UNCONDITIONAL STROKES

Many of the strokes we received in our very early years were unconditional. Parents and others around us cuddled us, did special things for us, and said such things to us as, 'You're smashing' or 'It's so wonderful to have you'. In many ways we experienced unqualified appreciation. We had to do nothing to earn the strokes, nothing as a consequence, and were not told what to do if we wanted more. They were straightforward, unconditional, appreciative strokes for us simply as we were.

Many other strokes, however, were used to exert some influence over us to make us more like the way other people wanted us to be. Strokes have always been used as a way of shaping behaviour, and whole schools of psychology have been based on operant conditioning, behaviour modification, and positive reinforcement. As experienced by the child, conditional strokes are likely to be saying either, 'I will like you if you behave like this', or 'I will value you if you achieve this'. Conditional strokes are mostly concerned with behaviour or achievement. We need to check whether our own mix of strokes, given and received, is particularly skewed towards unconditional, behaviour – conditional, or achievement – conditional, and what the consequence of that is.

Whereas positive unqualified strokes generally feel better than conditional ones, the reverse is true of negative strokes. There is not much you can do with a statement 'I hate you', but 'I really dislike the way you never help people here' does offer some opportunities of movement.

STROKES FOR OUR EGO STATES

We receive and give strokes for different ego states. People stroke our Nurturing and Controlling Parent, our Adult, our Adapted and Free Child. All need appreciation for their healthy operation, but we may, indeed commonly do, feel that one or other of our ego states gets less attention and others might be relatively over-stroked. In our relationship with others, we can check whether our strokes are nearly all given to one ego state or whether we appreciate all parts of the person. Only to express appreciation of someone's appearance and sense of fun may be very limiting for them and even be seen as persecutory.

GIVING, RECEIVING, ASKING FOR, REJECTING

We can look at any particular relationship, and indeed our whole life, by analysing the relative proportions of the strokes we give, receive, ask for and reject, both in positive and negative mode. This can be done by a visual display in the following manner (see **Figure 23**).

Key points raised for an individual may be:
- Why do I give many more positive strokes than I receive?
- Why do I receive more negative strokes than positive ones?
- Why do I ask for so few positive strokes?
- Why do I reject positive stokes, but not negative ones?

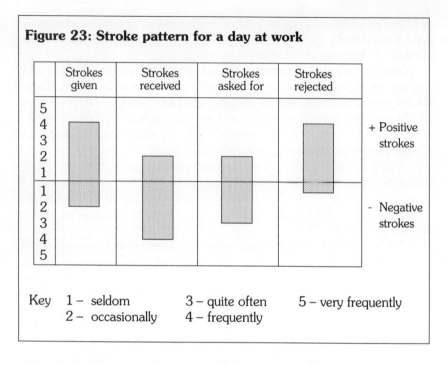

Figure 23: Stroke pattern for a day at work

	Strokes given	Strokes received	Strokes asked for	Strokes rejected	
5					+ Positive strokes
4					
3					
2					
1					
1					- Negative strokes
2					
3					
4					
5					

Key 1 – seldom   3 – quite often   5 – very frequently
     2 – occasionally   4 – frequently

Strokes are asked for both consciously and unconsciously, blatantly and subtly. A person may ask her partner, 'Do you love me?' This will generate a stroke of some sort. Equally she may say 'I love you' on the safe assumption that the response will be 'I love you too'. Some people are comfortable in asking for strokes outright, and will be frequently asking the equivalent of 'what do you think of it so far?' Others find it very difficult to ask for strokes for themselves, though very willing to give them to other people. For anyone who feels stroke-starved in some part of their being, a simple remedy is to ask for more. For example, the person whose Free Child state is the only one stroked by her colleague might start asking for strokes for the quality of work she is doing. The person whose Nurturing Parent ego state is heavily stroked might ask for a cuddle for his Free Child.

DISCOUNTING

Discounting is the term used for rejecting strokes. We do not have to accept a positive stroke, and if in full awareness we are clear we do not want a particular stroke, we are right to reject it. This is different from the process of discounting, which is a mechanism of putting ourselves down by not accepting good statements or deeds. We may do this because we have been taught to be modest and never publicly accept praise, or because we find it difficult to believe good about ourselves. Either way, we lose unnecessarily a gift that would nurture our growth and self-identity.

In theory it is easy enough to accept a positive stroke. All we need to do is to say 'Thank you' or 'I really appreciate that' and look as though we mean it. In fact we have enormous temptations to discount in some of the following ways.

Apply it to the giver

'You handled those employers very well, Samia.'
'Oh, but not nearly as well as you would have done.'

Apply it elsewhere

'Congratulations on getting your Master's, Joan. It must have been very hard work.'
'Well, I owe it all to my parents really.'

Globalise it

'You've done a really good job on this project. I know it was a tricky one.'
'Yes, the team did very well. We all worked at it and no one let the side down.'

Don't see it or ignore it

'That was a good presentation from the principal, and I thought your question and comment at the end was very penetrating.'
'Yes, it was a good presentation'.

Reject it

'You did that very well.'
'No I didn't. I should have done it much better.'

Discount the source

'That was a terrific conference you organised, Malcolm.'
'You're bound to say that, James. You always support me.'

Unfavourable interpretation

'Sheila, that was the best meeting I've ever seen you chair.'
'What was wrong with last week's meeting then?'

Analyse it

'That was a nice thing the vice-principal said to you.'
'I don't understand. Why do you think she said it to me?'

Laugh at it

'That's the best analysis of that problem I've ever seen, Victoria.'
'What? Little old me? You must be joking.'

It is worth noting that a discounted stroke is a slap in the face to the giver. A stroke is a present, and a discount is a way of throwing the present back. A very quick way of improving a relationship is to start to accept strokes with joy.

STROKES AT WORK

The key to understanding the process of stroke patterns in the work is to understand the absolute importance of the following fact. We all spend our time trying to reproduce the experience of stroking from our childhood. Our early stroke patterns were the medium through which we learned about our value to others and therefore to ourselves, and which greatly influenced our self-identity. Not unnaturally, therefore, we try to reproduce those patterns in our adult existence at work and home so that we can reinforce that sense of reassurance and security.

What does this mean in practice for managers and employees?

We can consider, as examples, a few of the managers in a typical workplace.

One manager experienced relatively few strokes when he was a child. He was on short rations, and learned to live with that. As a consequence he gives very few strokes to the staff in his section. When people give him strokes he discounts them, and indeed hardly notices them. If they are unavoidable, then he becomes very embarrassed. Consequently his staff have learned not to give him strokes. His view is, 'If people get paid for the job, what else can they want? The job itself ought to give people enough satisfaction.' Just sometimes he feels cold and lost inside, but he quickly brushes that away.

A second manager received a lot of strokes as a child for performing well – for winning at games, and for coming top of the class – and she now believes she is valued by others and values herself to the extent that she is the best. She gives a lot of strokes to her staff to encourage them to perform to their full potential, and she just sees it as perverse to stroke people for any other reason. She believes you do no favours to anyone by being nice to them when their work is indifferent. For herself, it takes a long time to get over any failure. To miss a promotion or to lose in a battle with another section's manager over resources dents her self-assurance and self-valuing badly. What good is she if she cannot deliver?

A third manager came from a strict and carefully regulated home, where as a child he was loved and stroked so long as he behaved himself and did what he was told. He learned to understand what was expected of him, and could then be assured of plenty of strokes. He became acute at anticipating his parents' and teachers' expectations, and was often described as a very co-operative and responsible child. Now he continues to spend time anticipating other people's needs, and fitting in with what the organisation seems to want him to do. He strokes his own staff on the basis of their co-operative spirit and willingness to follow the rules. If he does suggest a new idea, and it meets any criticism, he quickly drops it. He doesn't want to be seen as a trouble-maker. 'Don't make waves' is his motto. Just sometimes he finds himself thinking he would like to do something outrageous that would shock everyone, but he soon pulls himself together and is ashamed of such thoughts.

A fourth manager had an unhappy childhood in which she was heavily criticised and often punished for making a mess of things. She often did things well, but these were ignored or if noticed at all her parents would find something wrong somewhere. She found at school that she attracted plenty of attention when she got things wrong, just like at home; and without realising it, whenever she needed some reassurance that others noticed her, she would mess something up. Now, she tends to set projects up that she then neglects, she forgets to send in important returns until it is too late, and her days are filled with crises. Her personal finances and relationships are also messy, and some of her friends feel very sorry for the bad time she is often having from the negative strokes of her colleagues and her manager. Occasionally she will think, this is stupid. I'm perfectly capable of handling everything that comes my way very well, but then she seems almost deliberately to mess up something else.

Two other managers work very closely together because they job-share. They are, however, finding it very difficult to get on together. Jocasta feels that Helen does not appreciate her or even like her very much. She notices that Helen never says much in the way of appreciation or thanks, and seems to take her for granted. 'It wouldn't hurt her just to say for once she likes working with me or even she likes me.' Helen, however, also feels very unappreciated. 'What has Jocasta ever really done for me to show that she values me?' In fact Jocasta very often gives Helen really good strokes by telling her how much she appreciates her work and her company, while Helen puts great thought into things she does for Jocasta – covering for her when the children were ill, getting her some information on a holiday deal, and the like. Jocasta's childhood experience was that you know you are valued when people tell you – without that, you cannot be sure. Helen's experience was that you can tell which people value you by seeing what they do for you – words are just words, but actions are real. For the two managers to improve their working relationship, Jocasta needs to give some strokes by actions occasionally, and Helen needs to say what she feels rather than rely only on doing things for Jocasta.

The reader, when familiar with the chapters on drivers and games, might consider each of the above cases and speculate on the most likely associated drivers and games.

STROKES AND THE COMPETENT MANAGER

The competent manager will probably have had a childhood which was rich in all the various kinds of strokes, and which were given to him or her from an OK state. Alternatively, the manager may have learned to compensate for past experience, and consciously use strokes skilfully and appropriately. This would require that he or she was able to:

 - use strokes frequently, not sparsely;
 - direct strokes to all the ego states of the recipient;
 - stroke via words, actions and touch as appropriate;
 - stroke unconditionally, and for behaviour and achievement;
 - avoid discounting strokes and challenge it in others;
 - ask for strokes when needed;
 - use positive strokes often, and negative ones seldom.

A change in the overall stroke patterns in an organisation can profoundly improve its climate and the effectiveness of the people within it. It is an enterprise which managers can essay in the development of their own skills. The analysis we have presented of game theory, rackets and stroke patterns, however, must include the caution that individual stroke patterns are woven into all aspects of our lives; and when we might appear to be contemplating a superficial change, this may in fact involve a fundamental reappraisal of the way we live our lives.

CHAPTER 9
SCRIPTS

WHAT IS A SCRIPT?

Our script conditions our lives. It is the basis on which we live out our days. It determines much of our behaviour, our images of ourselves and others, our dreams, ambitions and expectations. Our script is formed when we are very young. It is in the process of being made from our birth up to the age of seven or eight. After that, though we may modify it in various ways, its main lines are set. We have by then come to some firm decisions about what we are like, what others are like, what life is all about, and what part we are going to play in it. Henceforth we are a captive of our script and dutifully play out our role. To reach greater freedom and autonomy we have first to understand what our script is, and secondly, to move out of script behaviour as often as we can.

How is a script formed in the first place? We need to try to remember back to our very early years – say when we were two. We have to think how small we are in a world full of big people, big furniture, big voices. In this world we constantly face all sorts of unpredictable and random events. We quite unexpectedly face the full force of bad and good feelings of other people. It is a confusing, frightening world, and we have to try to make sense of it to want to carry on with life at all. We want to find out what the rules are, what seems to work most of the time, what is expected of us, what life is all about.

However, at that age we are very vulnerable indeed in four particular ways:
- we are very weak and powerless, almost everyone is much stronger than we are;
- we are not able to deal with or tolerate high levels of anxiety or stress;
- we have only a rudimentary thinking capacity. Rational or logical thought is undeveloped, and wrong conclusions are easily drawn;
- we lack information. Our total sum of data is very restricted and very focused. Most information comes to us via our custodians, often heavily screened. In particular, we do not have sufficient information to compare the behaviour we see in our home with knowledge about what goes on in the rest of the world.

The child normally has no option about where she lives, and whom she lives with, but in the vulnerable state she is in has nevertheless to get by and make sense of what is happening around her.

The process of making sense of the world, of coming to decisions about it and her place in it, is what is meant by forming a script.

How does the child do this? Primarily by listening to the thousands of messages she receives about herself and others, and the world in which they live, and then trying to fit them all together. Not everything she hears will be worked into her script. Messages she hears will vary in frequency. If her mother says just once to her in exasperation, 'You are so stupid,' it will probably not be a significant part of the script. However, if the child hears this in some form or other every day, it will become an important part of her script. The potency of a message also depends on its source. The comments of the mother will be much more significant than those of a neighbour, or the big boy living down the road. Messages are also given with different emotional intensity, and it is the ones with a heavy emotional charge that are likely to make the most impact.

MECHANISMS FOR LEARNING SCRIPTS

There are three particular ways in which the child picks up messages about herself. These categories are not discrete, and many messages will spread across them, but they illustrate the particular mechanisms at work.

Modelling

The child has various behaviours modelled for her by the significant adults in her life. The behaviours often give clear and consistent messages. For example, she might see a father who works very hard and takes little time for his own enjoyment. She might well draw a message from this that being a man is a serious business, whose role in life is to work hard and support his family. She might see her mother give way to her father in every argument, and so decide women shouldn't stand up for themselves. Modelling is particularly concerned with sex scripting, but also affects all other scripting such as adult-child modelling which says, 'Tis what an adult is', and 'This is what a child is'.

Attributing

Each child must hear several times a day comments which describe him or attribute qualities to him. Anything that defines or labels the child in some way can be included in this category, e.g. 'You're bad, stupid, idle, careless, clumsy, thoughtless,' etc. 'You're just like your father,' 'You'll never be as bright as your brother,' 'You're not pretty but you're cute,' 'You're a lad,' 'A pity you're not strong like the others.' When these messages are heard day after day, and receive particular force through the circumstances during which they are said, or the intensity with which they are said, the child almost

74

inevitably has to come to a decision to believe he is like that – bad, stupid, clumsy, a drag like his father, etc. The messages do not, of course, have to be verbal. A father might give presents to his daughter which always reinforce the message, 'You're physically attractive,' and never 'You're intelligent'.

Suggesting

Adults can give to children clear indications of what they want or expect. For example, a child hearing frequently, 'Don't bother me,' might decide it is better to keep away from people unless he has been particularly good. A statement, 'Don't hang around me all the time,' might lead to a decision, 'I've got to make it on my own – they won't help me.' A statement, 'Nobody cares about me,' by a mother might lead a son to decide, 'I must give up my own needs, and stay around to look after her.'

MESSAGE TYPES

It is common sense that not all messages are harmful. Many are essential for survival in the world without hurt; others are the basis for development or growth in autonomy and creativity. Messages such as 'be yourself', 'believe in yourself,' 'enjoy the world,' 'give and receive love,' are all the kind of messages called permissions. They permit or allow the child to develop naturally, without artificially implanted limitations. He has maximum free choice and a chance to fulfil his potential. A child who receives plenty of permission messages will also be given a great deal of unconditional stroking. Indeed the unconditional stroke is the most powerful message to be yourself and value yourself. To separate these kinds of useful nurturing, caring and freeing messages from script messages, Shulamit Peck (in a UMIST seminar, 1973) refers to the first as the person's story and the second as the person's script. The former is allowing, the latter is limiting.

Script messages are most commonly in the form of injunctions or prescriptions. In whatever form they are expressed, they are likely to concern one of a very small number of crucial and basic messages that the child has to come to terms with. The following are the major crucial messages which can be given to the child, either as permissions or injunctions with various degrees of qualification.

Permission: exist
Injunction: don't exist

The basic message the child receives from the moment she is born is whether her parents want her around. If she is given strokes and acceptance, and valued for being there, she will want to live and belong, and will develop a sense of trust and optimism. If she is ignored, not handled or stroked as a baby and kept out of the way, she will only have a tentative drive to live, and feel her life is not worth anything. This message is often transposed into permission: be healthy and strong; injunction: be weak, die.

A child can receive messages that she is weak, susceptible to illness, likely to catch everything that is going around. The unstated message probably is, 'You are going to die' (I want you to die). If this is incorporated into script decisions, such people who have a potential for a healthy life no different to anyone else, will grow up plagued with illness and an ever-present concern about ill-health. Many of her activities will help her achieve an ill-health script rather than a healthy life, through bad eating habits, smoking, avoidance of elementary health precautions, restricted breathing, etc. Most children are given permission to grow up healthy and strong, and set about doing that.

Permission: feel and express emotions
Injunction: don't feel

If children are allowed freely to laugh, cry, feel anger, frustration and fear without script messages, they grow up feeling comfortable in having and expressing a wide range of emotions. If such expressions of feeling are suppressed by parents in childhood, children learn to discount and distrust their emotions and feelings. Such messages as 'boys don't cry', 'of course you're not frightened,' and 'don't shout so much,' will cause such discount. Instead of genuine and appropriate feelings, children learn to substitute the feelings their parents are prepared to approve of or at least live with. Such substitute feelings are racket feelings.

Permission: have and be aware of physical sensation
Injunction: don't feel sensations

Children will naturally learn to use all their senses – visual, kinesthetic, auditory, olfactory, and gustatory. Children may not receive permission to fully acknowledge sensations. Instead the messages they receive may be not to feel hunger or pain, not to see ('don't stare,' 'concentrate on what you are doing'). Such a person grows up detached and split off from her body and its sensations.

Permission: think
Injunction: don't think

The child needs permission and encouragement to think for himself, to develop his Adult ego state. Parents who encourage and value their child's ideas, questions, interests, enthusiasm, curiosity, and creativity, allow the child to feel it is OK to think for himself. If his attempts to think are discounted by ignoring, making fun of or putting down, then the child will grow up with a clear message that it is not a good thing to think for himself and trust his mind.

Permission: be close to others
Injunction: don't be close, don't belong

The growing child needs messages, particularly non-verbal and modelled, that it is OK to be physically and emotionally close to others. If the child is not cuddled and stroked, if parents are remote to him and each other, he may grow up with an injunction to be distant from people. He will experience difficulty in belonging. This injunction can be caused by the departure or death of a parent; when the child learns that it doesn't pay to get too close, because in the end you only get hurt or let down.

Permission: be who you are
Injunction: don't be you

The child needs confirming messages that her physical appearance as it develops is accepted by her parents. Every child learns quickly which sex she is and whether it is approved of by her parents. Her messages may be that boys are more valuable, or a boy may learn that he is the wrong sex because his mother wanted a girl. Approval or criticism of shape ('You're growing fat like your father'), of height ('All the rest of your brothers are tall'), colour, hair, eyes, legs, etc. are given in hundreds of messages to children. Discounting messages lead to a script with a powerful injunction against being as you are.

Permission: be your age
Injunction: hurry and grow up, or don't grow up

Messages given to a child may be to grow up quickly because parents are unhappy with young children, or want to be on their own, or don't want the financial burden. In such cases the child gets a message that it is not OK to be a child, needy and dependent on others, and finds it difficult to be carefree and playful. Conversely, parents may not want their children to grow up because they feel good when they have someone to look after and be dependent on them, or because they fear what nasty things will happen to their child through puberty and beyond. A child may get both messages – don't be a child needing our care and energy, but don't grow up and be independent and leave home. The script message to stay at home and take care of the parents is a very powerful one. Children need permission to be and enjoy the age they are, and also to go back to behaviours from previous ages on occasion. All ages anyone has lived through are good ages.

Permission: succeed
Injunction: don't make it

To give a child strong messages to succeed can be done in many ways – by encouragement, attribution, modelling, etc. Conversely, parents who put limitations and obstacles in a child's way, who feel jealous towards her, or pass on their own incapacity to work for their own success, will limit their child's capacity to develop an inner sense of competency. She will feel afraid or guilty of success. Some messages of this type relate to siblings – for example, not letting a younger brother go to grammar school because the elder failed, or not letting a daughter stay in the sixth form because the son was an academic failure. It is very difficult to have permission to succeed if the child has been given any of the previous eight injunctions – e.g. succeed but don't think, don't be close to others, don't exist, etc.

WHERE DO THE MESSAGES COME FROM?

Messages are not given by parents with carefully calculated malice nor are they given randomly. They are given out of the parents' own scripts. It is useful to distinguish the individual scripts of parents from those they carry by virtue of their position or status, and these latter we will look at first.

Ethnic or cultural script messages

A good many messages are given to children because they belong within a given ethnic or cultural group. The parent is the transmitter on behalf of his or her ethno-cultural group. Many messages relate to being Jewish, Welsh, Afro-Asian, Australian, Sikh, Geordie, Baptist, etc. Many of these messages will concern national identity, age scripting, sex role, religious belief and observance, and stereotyping of other ethnic/cultural groups.

Socio-economic class script messages

Many messages are related to socio-economic class, and help establish for the child, class identification and behaviour. These are often related to manners of dress and speech, and also to political orientation.

Family messages

Some families have a very strong family script, which all the members over the years try to pass on to their children. Typical script messages are:
'Our family is always in trouble with the police.'
'We've looked after the village for generations.'
'We've always had one black sheep in the family.'
'No one tells a Blackwood what to do.'

'We've never asked for help from anyone.'

Often, a parent will pass on the family saga or myth:

'We've been working our way up in the world for generations.'

'Grandad was a foundling – but he made a fortune.'

'We used to be gentry once.'

Very often related to this, though it might more properly come under the next section, is the vocational message. Many children get very strong messages about what they should become, either generally, e.g. 'You go to university and get on in the world,' or specifically, e.g. 'We've always been doctors in this family,' or 'You'll make a splendid parson,' or 'You'll be a docker like your Dad.'

Individual parents' messages

The majority of messages, however, are those that are consistently given, week after week, year after year, by the grown-ups in our lives. Some of these messages are good. They come from the OK part of the Parent, Adult and Child ego states, and help make the growing child a good Nurturing Parent, with a confident and clear-thinking Adult, a fun-loving Free Child, and an Adapted Child that is flexible enough to encourage good relationships and ease of living. Many of the messages are bad. They come from the not-OK part of our parents, and are a part of the script they were given when they were young. This script resides in the Adapted Child but might come out in the form of apparent parental injunctions and prescriptions. It is commonly called the Pig Parent, and the growing child is almost totally defenceless against it, while the grown-up may not even be aware of the way in which he is off-loading his own script and not-OKness into his daughter or son. In many of the TA textbooks, script matrices are drawn to demonstrate how the messages are passed on. The following matrix, illustrated by two messages, applies to a child aged two or three (see **Figure 24**).

As the child grows older, he develops a stronger Adult which is not dependent upon other people defining his thinking and reality for him, and an independent Parent which works out the rules and responsibilities he wants to live by. The script messages from childhood stay as tapes, however, and are firmly embedded in the Child ego state, though they will often come out as parental statements. The messages from the father's and mother's own not-OK Child are locked into the not-OK Child of their grown-up son and will emerge as tapes from his past either in his Child or not-OK Parent. The messages which have been useful, liberating, and allowing will have come from his father's and mother's OK ego states and will have helped their son form his mature Parent and Adult states.

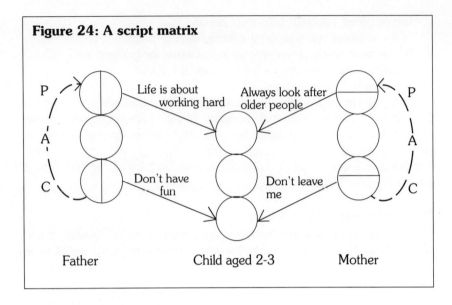

Figure 24: A script matrix

Life is about working hard

Always look after older people

Don't have fun

Don't leave me

Father   Child aged 2-3   Mother

FINDING OUT ABOUT SCRIPTS

Script analysis is a way of finding out and getting into some kind of order, the script messages you have received and are bound by. There is no standard process. Some TA workers use a questionnaire, others prefer using occasional stimulus questions and free association to see what comes up. It is useful to work with another person, changing roles halfway through the session. During such a session, the person working on his or her script must take prime responsibility for the activity – the other person is there as a facilitator, asking questions and making suggestions but is not responsible for analysing the other person's script.

At the start, it is useful to collect together all that you have learned about yourself from working through the other parts of TA. You may already know your stroke pattern, typical egogram, your stroke profile, your rackets and your games.

To start working back to your script messages you need to address yourself to such questions as the following:

- What do you remember or have been told about your grandparents?
- What kind of people are/were your mother and your father?
- What was the story of your birth? Who told you about it?
- Why were you called by your forename(s)?
- What is/was your nickname?

- When you think of your mother in your childhood, what is she doing and what is she saying to you?
- When you think of your father in your childhood, what is he doing and what is he saying to you?
- What did your parents want you to become?
- Think of when you felt really good with your father.
- Think of when you felt really bad with your father.
- Think of when you felt really good with your mother.
- Think of when you felt really bad with your mother.
- What was your favourite fairy story?
- Who was your favourite hero (male or female)?
- How old do you expect to be when you die?
- What will you die of?
- What will be written on your tombstone (and on the back of it)?
- Write down all the things you remember your parents passing on to you.

This last question needs some time given to it. Many of the things you remember will probably be parental advice or commands – e.g. keep your shoes clean, wash your hands, you can only do your best, look after your mother, don't interrupt, etc. Aim for about 30 items.

Lists of script questions can be found in many TA text books, but it is important to treat them simply as stimulus questions. You should not feel obliged to find an answer, nor keep your answer to the limits of the question asked. If you have no response to a question, then leave it. If, for example, you have no memories of any comments about your birth, then pass on to the next question, though do not be surprised if much later you suddenly remember a birth story buried deep in your memory. Allow answers to the questions to lead where they will by free association. You may find that three or four of these questions set off hours of remembered material which makes the remaining questions superfluous.

As you work through this material, the key elements in your script will start coming through loud and clear. You do not need to be a clever therapist to do this. All you need is persistence, common sense, a determination to be honest with yourself, and confidence in your ability to understand yourself better than anyone else can (although, as said before, it is beneficial to do it as a mutual activity with a peer). As tentative conclusions are formed about script messages, check them out with yourself and other people. If they feel right to you, then they almost certainly are right. During script analysis, it is important to be aware of the significance of the signs your body and speech will give – changes in breathing, a particular emotional charge on a specific word in a sentence. Nobody ever picks up all the clues, but most people with concentration and effort can pick up enough to discover the script messages that lie underneath.

PATTERNS OF SCRIPT

Many people's scripts fall into one of six patterns over their life span. The six major patterns are as follows.

The never script

This script binds a person never to get what he wants. He may talk about or start all sorts of projects, and he may try awfully hard, but he will never actually achieve what he wants – he never gets married, never becomes a doctor, never goes to America, never enjoys sex, never writes his book – in fact whatever he sets himself up to do, his script behaviour will make sure he fails to achieve.

The always script

This is the converse of the never script. A person with this script always feel constrained to carry on doing the same as she is doing now. Such a person may always stay at home looking after other people; always work in the same depressing job; always move about from place to place; or whatever particular role she has committed herself to performing for life.

The until (before) script

This script binds a person to defer his reward until certain other activities have been completed. Everything is conditional upon first accomplishing the appropriate labour. He might live a life full of self-denial and hard work to enjoy life in the hereafter; or work hard while the children are young, to enjoy life and have fun when they are off his hands.

The after script

Someone living out an 'after' script assumes that everything she now has that she enjoys, she will have to pay for in the future. If she has good health, illness will catch up with her later. If she is born into wealth, she will be made destitute some time in the future. She can never accept what she has now, without thinking what is to come after.

The almost (over and over) script

The 'almost' script binds a person almost to achieve what he wants, but always to fail at the final hurdle. He repeats over and over again his efforts to get there, and every time just fails. Such people almost get their degree, almost clinch the sale, almost break the record, almost buy a house.

The open-ended script

The open-ended script leaves a person with no direction after a certain part of her life is over. She is given a script to marry and bring up children, but no instruction of what to do when they are grown up. So she loses any orientation and purpose in life when that happens. She may be scripted to work hard to get a good education, but is lost once she has gained her PhD, or to have a dynamic career, and feels life is at an end when she retires.

Most people tend to approximate to one of these scripts, both in overall life plan, and in lifestyle as reflected in their daily business. Stan Woollams (Woollams and Brown 1978) gives some interesting examples of how sentence construction in conversations varies according to these scripts. There are some people who live one pattern of script at work, and another at home – for example, an open-ended pattern at work and an 'until' pattern at home.

What to do with your script

As the script is revealed, what can its owner do about it? Is script analysis nothing more than an academic exercise? Is there any stage beyond the self-knowledge that comes with it? There are two important points to make here.

Firstly, a script has no magical qualities. It is not a mysterious entity buried deep in the individual's psyche. It is no more and no less than the messages given by ordinary, everyday people to the young child and the decisions he made to cope with those messages. It is possible therefore to give yourself another set of messages to replace the original ones, and make a new set of decisions about your life. The movement from one set of messages, given in childhood, to another given in maturity, may not in practice be easy; because the first set were given with potency and absorbed by a vulnerable child and reinforced many times over the ensuing years. They have simply been around a long time. It might be necessary to utilise the help and strength that a TA group can give, or if you like expensive one-to-one relationships you could use a therapist. This can give the extra power and drive to compensate for the strength of the original messages.

Secondly, the decision of what to do with your life is yours alone. If you contemplate the script you have unravelled and decide it is not too bad to live with, then that is your right. No one has the right to tell you that you ought to change.

However, before you decide to stay as you are, it is worth thinking about one of Eric Berne's fundamental insights. In a pointed phrase he describes the baby as being born a prince or princess. It has no script. Its position is one of basic trust in the world. Before the child has been worked over by the people around him, he is a being capable of unqualified love, of spontaneous joy, and of straight thinking. It is the script which has twisted, perverted, limited, and destroyed those capacities in the grown adult, and it is the rediscovery of that potential which is the reward for those who begin to destroy their scripts.

NAMING

There are two avenues into script exploration which frequently lead to particularly rich insights and so are dealt with in some detail. The first is the use of naming and birth stories. The second is the use of fairy tales.

Throughout the history of human experience names and naming have been thought very important; incorporating magical, religious, political and traditional elements. Myths, folk tales and fairy tales are repositories of stories about the potency and magic of names: for example, that-which-cannot-be-named without harm falling on the namer, the riddle of a name that must be guessed if disaster is to be avoided, the power of the individual that is intact so long as no one can name him, are common in most folk cultures throughout the world. People's relationships with their names are complex and deep and we would be wrong not to pay attention to it in any kind of psychological analysis.

Certainly, naming of children is today treated as a matter for considerable thought and much energy goes into it. Hundreds of thousands of books which list forenames and their meanings are sold year by year. Many couples will go through a long and absorbing process of selection, working from a short-list to the final selection. Along the way there may be furious disagreements that need to be sorted out. The father and mother may disagree, friends may be drawn into the dispute. The name chosen may cause pleasure to kin whose name has been taken or annoyance to those whose expectations have been disappointed.

Once we are given our forenames, that is not the end but the beginning. As we move into different circles from our family to school friends, work-mates, social acquaintances and lovers, there is creative play made on our name. Names are shortened, nicknames invented, alternative names ascribed and lovers' names whispered. Variations on names can come from affection, dislike, malice and many other feelings. Most people acquire quite a number of variations and alternatives to their names.

Given the potency of names, we can consider what part they have played in forming and reinforcing our scripts. What were our parents saying to us when they chose our names? What lay behind the choice? What stories are there about your naming? What did they subsequently do with the names?

You can work through the following questions relating them to the giving of your own names but you can also use them to analyse the name-giving of your own children.

Naming questionnaire

	Is this significant?	How do you feel about it?
1 Have you been given a family name i.e. a parent's, grandparent's, or other relative's?		
2 Were you told that your parents knew what they wanted to call you well before your birth – or that they still couldn't think of a name until the last minute?		
3 Did your parents originally intend to call you something else but changed their minds?		
4 Did your parents make a mistake when your name was registered – getting the name or the spelling wrong?		
5 Were you given one forename or two or more than two?		
6 How feminine, masculine or androgynous is your name? If a female name, is it a feminised version of a male name?		
7 Were you named after a famous person, e.g. member of the Royal Family, film star or footballer?		
8 Is your name very common, unusual, one-off?		
9 Is your name plain or ornamental?		
10 Were you called one version of your name by your parents and another by your friends, e.g. does your mother always call you William even though everyone else calls you Bill?		
11 Do you have a name that embarrasses you?		
12 Do you commonly use your second (or third) rather than your first name?		
13 Did your parents use a shortened version or pet name for you?		
14 What did your school friends call you – and those really close to you?		

The birth story

Naming is often inextricably linked with the birth story. Many children become aware of a story attached to their birth. It may have been mediated to them very subtly, and it may be something they have intuitively sensed rather than have been told. Such stories can be very powerful script influences indeed. Consider, for example, one woman who became aware as a child that her mother had been in labour for two days, had nearly died, and had been ill for several weeks afterwards. What kind of sense can the child make of that? One way might be for her to decide that she had nearly killed her mother and nothing she could ever do would make up for that.

Which of the following fits you? What I felt or heard as a child (and later as an adult) was that I was:
- a special gift to my parents;
- an extra burden to an already overstretched family;
- a problem to my parents' plans;
- a mistake (the word we often use for unplanned pregnancies);
- a carefully planned event;
- a disappointment (generally the wrong sex);
- a late arrival – either over time or late in child-bearing life;
- an early arrival – either premature or early in child-bearing life;
- a cause of pain or illness.

What I sensed of the feelings of my parents about my birth were of:
- joy,
- pain,
- excitement,
- illness,
- endurance,
- death,
- disappointment,
- annoyance,
- fear.

It is worth noting that when looking at the script issues of birth and naming stories we are not concerned with accurate, historic fact. The importance is on what you heard or intuitively felt when you were a child, and to some extent subsequently as an adolescent and adult. Your understanding may have been partial or erroneous but if that is what you thought was reality, then it was the reality for you, and was a part of your script formation.

FAIRY TALES

Why do we pay attention to people's experience of fairy tales in working with their script?

Firstly, our experience of fairy tales nearly always takes place in our childhood when our script is being formed. They were among the earliest tales we heard; so the way in which we selectively heard them and made decisions about which we liked best, which frightened us, which we made part of our imaginative lives in the way children do, which did nothing for us and we consigned to an imaginary dustbin, are all questions which are worth exploring.

Make a list of your favourite fairy tales. Note any particular scenes that seem to come into your mind automatically – those that are associated with good feelings and those associated with fright or distaste.

Fairy tales are believed by many psychologists and therapists to have a potency, to create a depth of experience in the child, way beyond the children's stories or TV series which are also part of childhood. This is because they are genuine folk tales coming out of a centuries-old oral tradition which preserved only those poems, tales and myths which had a function for the development of the identity of the growing child within the community. Fairy tales help the child to solve the existential problems he or she faces. In particular they help the child to answer the three basic script questions:

- What is the world really like?
- How am I to live my life in it?
- How can I truly be myself?

The fairy tale has a structure which enables it to be used by the child at many levels. It is always multi-layered in its meaning, enabling the child to find answers at his or her own level of comprehension. So it is useless to ask what is the meaning of a particular fairy tale? The child at different ages facing different existential problems will find appropriate meanings.

Apart from having multi-layered meanings, the fairy story always has one quality – that of a happy ending. (This makes one or two of Anderson's tales not fairy tales in the real sense.) This is what is so important for the child in coming to terms with script issues. It says that whatever the present difficulties and painful experiences, in the end it can all come right. It is this belief in the ultimate happy ending that enables children to think out their present problems – whether it is of sibling rivalry, separation anxiety, rejection by the mother or persecution by the father. This is also what distinguishes the fairy tale from the myth. Myths do not necessarily have happy endings although they often have glorious ones. Myths are about great heroes whom we could try to emulate, not always successfully. Their activities are on a grand cosmic scale, and we are always going to feel inferior to them. Not so with the fairy tale which is homely, which makes no demands on the child, but gives reassurance and hope for the future, offering ways of working out the difficulties that are being faced now. Lewis Carroll referred to 'the love-gift of the fairy tale', and that is a very good way of distinguishing it from the myth. The myth is hardly a love-gift to the child.

What the fairy tale does so effectively is to externalise the inner, and often unconscious, fears, contradictions and chaotic feelings and thoughts of the young child. How does the child deal with the alternating love and hate it has towards the mother who is sometimes loving and sometimes rejecting (as all mothers are). In the fairy tale, the maternal force splits into the all-good and the all-evil mother. How does the child deal with its fear of having to separate from symbiosis with the parents and develop its own autonomous being? In the fairy story, children are abandoned or go off into the forest. How do children deal with the physical fear of grown-ups? In the fairy story, the young girl or boy outwits the giant. How do children develop beyond instant gratification of their physical needs, particularly oral gratification? In the fairy story, greed of the child leads to terrible situations (as in Hansel and Gretel). Whatever the issue, and at whatever level the child can understand and work with it, the fairy tale offers a reassurance in the child's powerlessness, of help being available at the critical times. The message is:

that a struggle against severe difficulties in life is unavoidable, is an intrinsic part of human existence – but that if one does not shy away, but steadfastly meets the unexpected and often unjust hardships, one masters all obstacles and at the end emerges victorious (Bettelheim 1976).

So we can summarise the fairy tale thus:
- It helps the child bring order from the chaos of its own inner life, relating to its unconscious problems. It deals with the child's inner reality and satisfies the need to find ways to externalise that inner life.
- It offers a view of the world which, though full of trials, has a happy ending. It enables the child to cope with his feelings of powerlessness and imagine a world in which magical helpers and radical transformations can take place. But although this is a wondrous world in which the child can outwit the giant and evil witch, there is always a return to reality at the end.
- The fairy tale does not insist on one moral lesson as in parables and fables but invites the child into situations where the learning is available within the child's comprehension.
- The fairy tale addresses all the great dilemmas of childhood – working through oedipal issues, learning to distinguish the reality principle from the pleasure principle, handling rage and destructive wishes, experiencing love-rejection from parents, sibling rivalry, fears of separation, the challenge of leaving the symbiotic parent relationship (leaving home) and sexual awakening.
- The most common devices psychologically in fairy tales are splitting, projection and symbolic substitution. (Examples of these – the good fairy and the bad fairy which splits the mixed nature of the parent into

two separate beings, so the good stays uncontaminated in the child's mind. Projecting on to the wicked stepmother the destructive urges it feels towards its own mother. Substituting a dragon or a giant for the fearsome adult.)

Such a rich source of the imaginative world of our childhood must have importance in the forming of our script. By working on those fairy tales which had great interest for us when we were children, we can get in touch with some of the powerful experiences from which script decisions were made. The following offers no more than a suggested guide for getting started .

Working with the fairy tale

Choose the one or two fairy tales which particularly attracted you when you were a child, and which you liked hearing over and over again. Then also choose the one you really disliked and were careful to avoid. These are the tales to work on.

Write out a synopsis of the plot, forgetting it is a fairy tale. Just treat it as an incident, and use matter of fact language, for example – a girl was told by her mother to go through a dangerous wood to take some provisions to her grandmother. She was given a bright red coat to wear, but told to keep to the path and beware of strangers. She stopped to pick flowers, and was accosted by someone she failed to recognise as a wolf.

Now look at the story you have written and complete the following sentences for yourself:
- What now surprises me about it is ....
- What I notice particularly interesting about it is ....
- The contradictions in it are ....

Take each of the characters in turn and ask yourself whom they stood for in your childhood, e.g. the giant, the wicked witch, the king etc.

Now imagine yourself as you were when a child, and imagine yourself into each of the roles in the story. Note whether the feelings in the roles correspond to feelings you remember having as a child – whether malevolent, benevolent, confused.

Think of the wicked characters and imagine them as the bad side of someone you loved in childhood – then join them together with the good side – e.g. the bad and good fairy, the cruel stepmother and the good mother.

Imagine yourself as one of the props in the tale – the beanstalk, the clock in Cinderella, the basket in Little Red Riding Hood, or whatever you choose. Then ask yourself what you see, what you hear, what you feel.

Look at any incidents which you remember as being both frightening and fascinating, and ask what it signified about your feelings, particularly those difficult to acknowledge.

What situations in the story have parallels with your own childhood? Look at such things as relationships with parents and siblings, abandonment, separation, favouritism.

What general themes or morals in the stories do you think became part of your script?

Look for any relationship between your racket feelings and drivers and the story.

Tell the tale and begin to play with it creatively – reverse things, let events happen back to front, change objects into other objects, make the good bad and the bad good, the weak powerful, the strong weak. Don't stay with your inventions too long unless you find out something worth exploring. Just move to another bit of play. But always retell to yourself the original version of the fairy tale at the end.

All these points are simply ways of exploring your childhood and your script. If they do not lead anywhere, then pass on to the next. You are looking for 'Aha!' insights.

CHAPTER 10

ORGANISATIONAL SCRIPTS

We can hardly fail to notice how different the various organisations are that we work in during our lives, nor fail to be aware of similar differences in those organisations we peripherally encounter. The whole feel and atmosphere of our own organisation is special to that place, and distinct from any other. Organisation theorists who examine this phenomenon have used various devices for analysis; most commonly in the last few years that of organisational culture derived from anthropological methodology. An alternative is the metaphor of the script, applying it to organisations in a similar way to which it is applied to individuals. We can think of the many organisations we have experienced in our lives, as analogous to our friends and acquaintances over the years; and just as the latter have their different scripts based on their unique history, the messages they heard and the life decisions they made, so can we perceive the script of our schools, colleges and offices.

It is important to emphasise that this is a metaphor, rather than assuming the organisation is an actual sensing and thinking body. An organisation is a social construct, and the actuality is that individual people are operating in fairly predictable and patterned ways, to achieve some agreed common purposes through some kind of contract. Using metaphors is a way of gaining extra insights. If in a college or school the staff feel constrained in various ways by the place; or if there seems some kind of limitation on the freedom of action that would seem to be functionally appropriate; or if there seems to be a 'hidden hand' or force influencing the organisation, then the metaphor of the script should help in our analysis.

Firstly, it is useful to think of some of the broad differences between organisations. In one college everyone behaves, assumes, takes it for granted that it is very successful and will continue to be so – there is a general air of optimism, a belief that the college can deal with any problems that come its way and achieve even greater success in the future.

In another college there may be a general air of aggression, the feeling that everyone is the enemy and unless the staff are very watchful and wary, they will be done down by rivals from outside. Internally this might be reflected by a sharpness or over-competitiveness between departments, post holders, or even in the mundane everyday encounters of individuals.

In a third college, there is a pervasive feeling of failure. Things seldom seem to go right for very long, staff assume that crises are always just round the corner, and there is no great faith in the capacity of the managers to improve the performance of the college.

A fourth college might be just jogging along, nobody trying very hard for improved standards nor failing very badly to reach average performance. There is low energy, lack of excitement, general banality.

Although any actual college would present a much richer picture, these four stereotypes (and a few more besides) should evoke common recognition among college and school staff.

What has caused the differences? Why are these organisations living out different scripts?

SOURCES OF THE SCRIPT

Some of the key influences in the early formation of the school or college script are as follows.

The founding fathers (or mothers)

Just as in the individual script the parents or surrogates are very powerful influences, so in organisations are the figures who founded and led the body in its early years. Generally, this will be the first principal or head teacher, but it might be a particularly powerful chairman of governors or benefactor. These figures gradually pass into the history and traditions of an organisation and around them are often built a whole complex of stories and anecdotes, some no doubt apocryphal, but all serving the purpose of defining the kind of place it is.

Organisations can be compared to the biological life of a human being but we must not be confused by the comparison. Organisations do not have a genetic timer ticking away which will lead to death and dissolution in a determined range of years, if catastrophe does not strike earlier. Organisations are socially constructed and do not need to die. They will simply cease to be supported when they no longer serve any function. So it is common for schools and colleges to experience periodic rebirths when a charismatic new leader takes over and revitalises the place. Such a leader will, in turn, become one of the great influences on the script and in time becomes the object of more myths and stories.

National, cultural and local influences

As with the individual whose script is partly shaped by the nation, culture, community and social class into which he or she is born, so the organisation's script will be defined by its community's expectations. At the macro level, it will conform to some general rules about what colleges are, what they should do, how they should appear, which are generally applicable across the country (although they would not necessarily apply in other countries or continents). At the micro level, agencies and bodies that are specific only to that college or school will be placing expectations on it to which it has to make some kind of response. It is worth emphasising the point made in the chapter on scripts that the organisation, like the individual, does not respond in a pre-determined way but makes idiosyncratic decisions about what is the best way to survive in these kinds of circumstances. So the school or college will hear messages from local employers, community bodies, from the local culture, from other schools and colleges. These messages, particularly if they are negative, are very powerful and difficult to discount. A school that is seen as in the 'wrong' street or district might be commonly referred to as one with difficulties, or a tough school. This then becomes part of its script.

Naming

Naming is part of scripting. The choice of name is something that sets up expectations and limitations at its foundation and with which it then has to live. Consider the effect of the following names:
- Bilston Mechanics Institute;
- Gem Street Elementary School;
- St Julian's Preparatory School;
- Cheltenham Literary and Scientific Institute;
- Cranleigh College, Oxford;
- Willington Technical College;
- Willington College of Art and Technology;
- Willington Community Youth and Sports Centre.

Just as individual nicknames are important, so is the name by which the school or college is familiarly called. The governors may have re-named it the –shire College of Art and Technology, but what is the significance if the locals all call it the tech? Nevertheless, part of the process of consciously changing the script may be to change the name.

Religious and philosophical influences

Colleges and schools are set in a philosophical, religious or educational setting. Sometimes this is very obvious. A Roman Catholic school or college is very clear about its purpose, its beliefs and the educational environment it wants to support. So is, for example, a Rudolf Steiner school. Some of the progressive independent schools such as Summerhill, Dartington or the Quaker boarding schools have had very distinctive practices and beliefs that are made absolutely clear to prospective clients. In other colleges the influence of the beliefs of a particular society or individual may be a less obvious, but nevertheless important, part of the script. This is true of many educational institutions set up by the Church of England. Local authority colleges and schools may respond to the general political tone of the authority, as was the case in many ILEA (Inner London Education Authority) institutions. Concern with the disadvantaged, with equal opportunities for women, ethnic groups and those with special needs from mental or physical impairment was much more overt than in most parts of the country.

Colleges and schools make choices, for whatever reasons, about the social, moral, religious and educational stances they wish to represent. One college might espouse a Thatcherite market philosophy and be responsive to whatever customers are there to buy their expertise. Another might see itself as part of the process of transforming society to one in which there is more equality and social justice. A third might be concerned to prepare its students for a period of further advanced study in higher education. Whatever the decision, the organisation will have developed a set of values and beliefs to support its choice. What we are witnessing here is the most fundamental of script decisions – the answer to the question 'Who am I?' The script is fundamentally about establishing a survivable identity and every organisation has to do this as much as every individual.

The statement of organisational identity and the values and belief system that support it may be incorporated in a founding charter, or an articulated vision, or a stated mission; or it may be that, like some unfortunate individuals, the school or college is confused about its identify and displays all manner of pathological behaviours as a consequence.

IDENTIFYING THE SCRIPT

As a first step to working out the script of an organisation, ask the following questions.

- What has been the influence of the founding figures and subsequent regenerative leaders?
- What are the national, regional, cultural and social class influences on the script?
- What is the significance of the name, any alternative name used in common parlance, and any formal name changes?
- What have been its religious, educational and philosophical beliefs? How has the place defined itself and supported that with value and belief systems?

Getting at the script

There is one very important question to ask. Is the organisation's a winning or a losing script? All the other questions are variants on this, although there are different ways of defining success.

Here are four suggested ways of exploring the script.

Organisational permissions and injunctions

As with the individual, the organisation needs to have accepted some basic assumptions about itself and to have avoided some key injunctions. These are adapted from the list in the previous chapter on scripts. There are eight key permissions.

Existence

The organisation needs to believe that it is OK to exist. Many schools and colleges don't ever question their right to exist, but others may have partially accepted the injunction 'don't exist' – so have as part of their script a belief that the organisation will probably cease to exist. In one city, for example, a college manager said, 'There has always been one too many colleges here, and we are constantly fighting for our life.'

Strength

The organisation needs to believe it is OK to be strong and in good condition. Most schools and colleges are probably only too glad to believe that, but some may have taken on the injunction 'don't be strong' – so they are inclined to believe their lot is to be weak and unhealthy.

Uniqueness

The organisation needs to feel it is OK to be the kind of place it is, and to resist injunctions that suggest it ought to be like other places. This can apply both to the type of institution and its unique place among similar institutions. For example, a technical college might feel it would be better as a higher education college; a comprehensive school that it would be better as a selective school. And the primary school might feel it would be OK if it were more like the primary school across town.

Achievement

The organisation needs to believe it is OK to be successful, to be the leader of the pack, the front runner, by whatever criteria it wants to be judged. It may have ingested an injunction, however, that it is likely to fail at what it tries to do, or at least never be particularly outstanding. Indeed being very successful may be seen as risky and uncomfortable.

Beliefs and values

The organisation needs to believe it is OK to feel strongly about things and stand up for what it believes in. The contrary injunction leads to organisations that are timid and worried about what others think of them, and will not go out on a limb for anything.

Reflection

The organisation needs to believe that it is OK to be a reflective and deep-thinking body, using all its capacity for analysis, creativity and intuition to learn from its experience and plan for its future. Some organisations believe the injunction, 'don't think and plan', and react blindly to events not knowing what they want or where they want to get to.

History

The organisation needs to feel comfortable with its age and its history, neither wishing to be a more ancient place with long traditions, nor last year's latest state-of-the-art creation. The injunction suggests to the college it ought to be newer and more vigorous, or older with more of a track record, but never the age it is.

Concern for others

The organisation needs to feel it is OK to be concerned for, sensitive towards, and friendly with other organisations. The counter injunction is to assume all outsiders are potential threats and good open relations with them are dangerous.

It is unlikely that any college or school will have totally incorporated any of the eight permissions or injunctions. In reality each institution will be on a continuum somewhere between the two extremes, and one with a healthy script will be towards the permission rather than the injunction side on most or all of the eight (see **Figure 25**).

96

Figure 25: The organisation's basic permissions and injunctions	
It's OK for the organisation to: or	The organisation:
exist	will probably fold up
be strong	will be weak
be the place it is	ought to be like others
be successful	will fail
feel strongly about things	will be timid and uncertain
be reflective	will act blindly
be the age it is	should be newer or older
work well with others	will be frightened of others

Patterns of scripts

We all have some concept of time in relation to ourselves, the way we imagine our past history on the one hand and our future on the other. We may see in our time-line all sorts of patterns. For example, we may be aware only of a misty past that is difficult for us to remember but a clear line stretching into the future; or we might see cycles that occur regularly – maybe starting with excitement leading through much investment and hard work to eventual disillusionment. Each person has his or her own unique way of seeing the time patterns of life, and this is true of organisations as well. We could all probably draw a line from one side of a sheet of paper to the other, to represent the ups and downs of our school or college's past experience. The script patterns described in the chapter 9 are here adapted to organisations.

The never script

This organisation is the one that never gets what it wants. It may talk a lot about it, set up planning meetings, designate staff to organise it, but somehow it never seems to get there. Whatever it sets out to do, it somehow finds a way of sabotaging.

The always script

This organisation is one that always carries on in the same way. No matter what changes occur outside, no matter what new challenges need to be faced, the organisation relies on the same processes, the same systems and structures, the same answer to problems.

The until script

In this organisation, brighter times are just ahead. For the present, everyone must buckle down and work extra hard because nothing worthwhile ever comes easily, but at some time in the future the school or college will reach its pot of gold at the end of the rainbow. This pattern is carried on year after year, so the hard sacrificing work is always there, and brighter times are always in the future.

The after script

In this organisation, staff are always nervous when things are going well, because good times always have to be paid for in the future. There is always a black cloud coming along behind the silver lining. So, if this year the student results are very good, the feeling will be that they are due for some bad intakes. If the reputation of the place is high, then a scandal will probably destroy it. If the principal is really good, then the next one will probably be awful.

The almost script

This organisation is one which almost achieves what it wants but fails at the last hurdle. It almost gets approval for a new course, is almost selected for a prestigious national pilot scheme, is almost chosen for a large benefaction, but somehow or other it always loses out in the final push.

The open-ended script

This organisation is the kind which has no sense of purpose or direction after a certain period of its existence is over. For example, a college might have known what it was about when it was primarily a part-time day release vocational college serving local industry, but now that is past, it feels the real life of the college is over. Or a school might have known where it was going as an 11-18 comprehensive but lost a sense of purpose when it became an amalgamated sixth form college. This time pattern is very similar to a Golden Age pattern, in which the staff constantly look back to a previous epoch when everything was fine, and compare it with the unsatisfactory present. The college or school identifies not with what now exists, but with a protected vision from the past.

Staff can check their own organisations against each of these patterns and assess whether that part of the organisation's script is helpful or harmful.

Script decisions

Each college or school will have come to some script decisions, by whatever conscious or hidden means, which seem to make sense of its place in the world around it. One way of checking these decisions is to work through a series of opposites and locate the college's position via **Figure 26.**

Figure 26: My organisation is the kind of place which:

 1 Tends to fail ....is a success
 2 Was once great......................developed from humble beginnings
 3 Competes vigorously ....is inward looking
 4 Is dedicated...........................is casual
 5 Takes care of people ....cheers up people
 6 Is friendly ....is impersonal
 7 Is self-centred.......................is concerned
 8 Is prudent ....:........................is improvident
 9 Is open.................................is secretive
10 Is tight-lipped ....is emotional
11 Is serious ....is fun
12
13
14
15

Try to add another four opposites which have significance for your organisation.

Having identified where your college stands in relation to these 15 qualities, analyse your responses by asking the following four questions:
- Where did these organisational characteristics come from?
- Are these messages any longer useful ?
- If you could change the script, what new messages would you want to adopt ?
- When are you going to do that ?

The fairy tale analogy

As indicated in chapter 9, fairy tales are useful aids to thinking about people's scripts. If you find this type of analogous thinking useful, consider what fairy tale your college or school represents.

Is it Cinderella, who always gets left to do the drudgery while the others go to the ball? Is it waiting for a fairy godmother to change the situation?

Is it Jack the Giant Killer, full of courage but not very good at planning ahead, and relying on quick wits and fleetness to foot to win over the powerful enemies it encounters?

Is it Sleeping Beauty, waiting for a prince to come and struggle through all the defences to bring everyone back to life with a kiss ?

Is it Little Red Riding Hood, wandering through dangerous forests very visibly with her goodies, unable to recognise a wolf when she sees one?

Or maybe the college is better represented by:

- Babes in the Wood;
- Hansel and Gretel;
- Snow White; or
- Goldilocks and the Three Bears.

You may wish to use one of the ancient myths instead, such as some of the labours of Hercules, the Holy Grail Quest, or such Odyssean tales as Penelope and her weaving.

The implications of the choice can be worked through by referring to the sets of questions in chapter 9 on individual scripts and fairy tales.

SUMMARY

In this chapter we have been using a double metaphor: the script as a metaphor for how people make decisions about their lives and make sense of their experiences; and the individual as a metaphor for the organisation.

We repeat, we are not saying organisations can think for themselves and have a real personality, but that we understand more about our experiences as organisational members, if we sometimes think of organisations as if they had their own scripts.

The point of all analysis and reflection is to decide at the end that either things are OK the way they are, or that it is time for changes to be made. Script analysis is simply one way of reaching that decision point.

CHAPTER 11
PROCESS COMMUNICATION AND ORGANISATIONAL ADAPTATIONS

INTRODUCTION

Taibi Kahler's process model (1978) is concerned with the initial approach of one person to another. It increases awareness and options in making contact, and is therefore particularly valuable for teachers, counsellors, sales people, market researchers and so on. It will help prevent the all too common feelings of having got off on the wrong foot or of failing to make contact.

HOW PEOPLE MAKE CONTACT

When you first communicate with someone else, they can be contacted through one of three modes:
- feeling;
- thinking;
- behaving.

An example of a feeling approach might be, 'It's lovely to see you,' or 'I'm glad to meet you, I've heard so much about you.'

An example of a thinking approach might be, 'How did you get on with that problem today?' or 'Any more news from your architect?'

If on meeting someone we said, 'Let's go for a walk and we can talk on the way,' or 'What do you want to drink?', we are operating in the behavioural mode.

We can invite people to respond to us initially from a thinking state, from a piece of behaviour, an action, or from their feelings. If we sense that we have not hit it off with someone it is possible we have used the wrong contact mode or, more accurately, a mode with which the other person feels uncomfortable.

ASSESSING INDIVIDUAL PREFERENCE

How can we know which contact mode people prefer? Kahler used the following device (**Figure 27**).

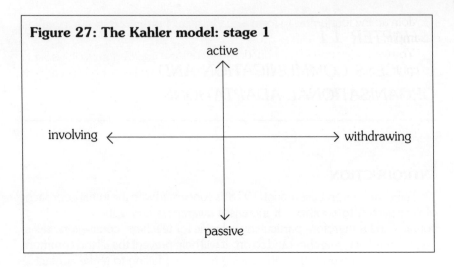

Figure 27: The Kahler model: stage 1

active

involving ← → withdrawing

passive

Complete the diagram for yourself by, firstly, considering how you respond to goal achievement. Are you, for example, someone who sets a goal and achieves it, or are you someone who tends to wait and see? You may quite often display both tendencies – active and passive – and so will have a wide range; or you may be fairly consistent, leaning towards one or the other and so have a narrow range.

Secondly, consider how you generally are in your life on an involving or withdrawing scale – again putting two marks, this time on the horizontal axis. In relationships with people; are you someone who goes out to involve others, or do you have a tendency to stand back and keep yourself to yourself, bar one or two close friends? If you tend to behave in a very involved way in personal relationships, your marks will be towards the left of the axis. Similarly, if you do not get involved and keep yourself to yourself, your marks will be to the right of the centre point. Neither is better that the other, just different.

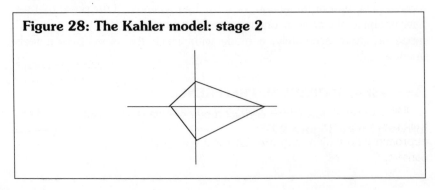

Figure 28: The Kahler model: stage 2

Join up the four points to form a quadrangle. **Figure 28** shows a worked example.

You will have a part of your quadrangle in all four quadrants but one is likely to contain a larger share than the others – one or two parts of the quadrant

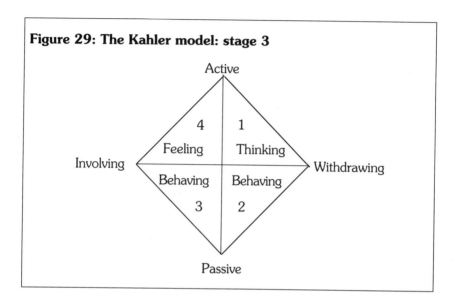

Figure 29: The Kahler model: stage 3

may have only a very small part of your quadrangle. This can now be related to the thinking/feeling/behaving modes (see **Figure 29**).

- Quadrant 1 – Withdrawn/active. The person strongest in this quadrant will, by preference, wish to engage first at a thinking level.
- Quadrant 2 – Withdrawn/passive. The person strongest in this quadrant will prefer to be approached in fairly passive behaviour. They will feel uncomfortable with a thinking or feeling approach.
- Quadrant 3 – Involving/passive. The person strongest in this quadrant responds most comfortably, initially to interactive behaviour with others.
- Quadrant 4 – Involving/active. The strongest response in this quadrant indicates the person is most comfortable in responding to feelings.

It is important to note that nearly all people can activate other modes than their dominant one when necessary. Their dominant mode determines the approach with which they are the most comfortable when making initial contact.

THE IMPORTANCE OF INITIAL CONTACT

Even though we move through a full repertoire of rich expression of feeling, thinking and behaving in any conversation, getting the initial contact right is critical. Just as a high point of stress is for the actor as he speaks his first words, for the musician as she plays her first note, so it is with human contact when the first words are spoken. They determine the quality of the subsequent interaction.

So, if we approached someone who was very strong in quadrant two (withdrawn/passive), shook their hand firmly and said, 'I want you to come over to meet some people,' they would feel very uncomfortable. Someone strong in quadrant three (involved/passive) would, however, probably welcome such a move to get them involved without much effort on their part.

AFTER THE INITIAL CONTACT

The initial contact can be very brief before moving on to another mode. One might say, 'Hello, are you feeling better today? Good. Now, I'd like your opinion on this report.' Paul Ware (1983) has suggested that there is a natural progression from the contact point to what he calls the target – full and extended communication. He also described what he called 'the trap', which is the mode most likely to panic or turn off the recipient if activated too early. His sequence theory is shown in **Figure 30**.

Figure 30: Process communication model

Quadrant	Contact	Target	Trap
1 Active/withdrawn	Thinking	Feeling	Behaviour
2 Passive/withdrawn	Behaviour	Thinking	Feeling
3 Passive/involving	Behaviour	Feeling	Thinking
4 Active/involving	Feelings	Thinking	Behaviour

EXPANDING THE MODEL

In order to understand the model better, we can fill it out with some other concepts.

Firstly, if it helps your thinking you can apply the following labels to each of the quadrants. (If it doesn't, don't.)

Active/withdrawn   —   workaholics,
passive/withdrawn   —   daydreamers,
passive/involvers   —   rebels,
active/involvers   —   overreactors.

Secondly, we can incorporate the drivers to the quadrants as shown in **Figure 31**. In the diagram, the drivers are displayed in a circle or a square. This is to distinguish between those drivers that are derived from an over-energised Parent (in squares) and those that are operating from the Adapted Child state (circles). It is a question of whether you are an over-adapter or an over-doer.

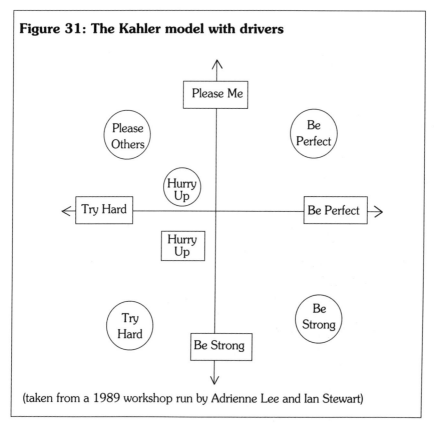

Figure 31: The Kahler model with drivers

(taken from a 1989 workshop run by Adrienne Lee and Ian Stewart)

Thirdly, we can add some script types to the model (**Figure 32**). As a reminder on script types:

- the **until** script. You cannot have fun and enjoy yourself until you have earned it by hard work and sacrifice;
- the **never** script. You will never get the things you really want;
- the **always** script. Things will always turn out the same;
- the **after** script. Whatever you enjoy or whatever good fortune you have, you will have to pay for it in the future;
- the **almost** script. You will nearly achieve all sorts of things but something always stops you in the end.

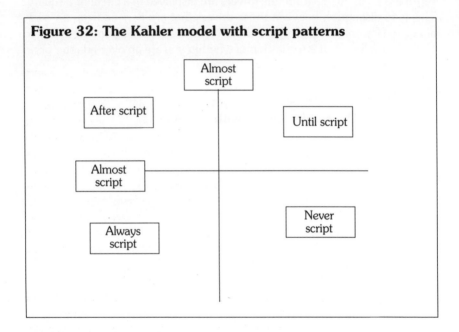

Figure 32: The Kahler model with script patterns

PUTTING IT TOGETHER

What does this mean when we interact with other people? What would improve the quality of communication?

If you are dealing with a workaholic (active/withdrawn), then an initial approach should be through her thinking mode. Her mind needs respect, her ideas listened to, and only then, when she is confident with you at that level can you switch into a feeling mode. For counselling or therapy that may be an important move, but for many purposes it is unnecessary to move from

106

the comfortable thinking mode. What the workaholic dislikes is feeling cornered, crowded or pressured. She will be anxious to talk but also keep her distance and will not like casual physical contact or taking part in 'party games'. She is likely to be driven by the need to get everything exactly right and this will be apparent in her speech patterns and probably in her appearance. She is likely to live a script which denies her any rewards or relaxation until earned by hard work and task completion.

If you are dealing with a daydreamer (passive/withdrawn), a gentle non-pressured approach is needed which allows him plenty of space and time. He is a loner, probably feeling driven to be independent of others and not to show his feelings. His script derives from his daydreaming, for he never seems to achieve anything that he really wants. From a low-key contact mode, you can move into a thinking mode with him, but the trap he is anxious to avoid is getting into communications about feelings. If you do ask him how he feels he will automatically answer 'fine' or 'OK', and then change the subject.

The rebel (passive/involver) has been alternately described by Vann Joines (**Transactional Analysis Journal**, 1986) as the charming manipulator or playful critic. She needs to be contacted through active behaviour, particularly some form of play. Once she is relaxed she can be contacted at a feeling level. It is very important for her that she is aware of her feelings before being faced with dealing at a thinking level on any issue. This person is likely to break rules but can always find a way of justifying her behaviour. People in this quadrant are sometimes described as slippery thinkers when under stress. Commonly we find Try Hard and Hurry Up drivers associated with such people, reflecting the priority they give to activity and feeling. Fundamentally however, their behaviour is repetitive. Their script can well be one in which they get into the same situation over and over again, and do not learn from the mistakes they keep making.

The overreactor (active/involver) is effectively contacted through his feelings and only when he has established relationships there can he move on to thinking about issues raised. The trap for him is being cornered into behaviour before he is completely relaxed with the relationship. He is inclined to be driven by the need to anticipate and fulfil the wishes of others around him, to please other people, and is often locked into a script which makes him feel that if he relaxes and enjoys himself he will have to pay for it later.

These are, of course, model types. None of us conforms to the extremes. We have a strong or weak tendency to be like one of the types but with a secondary type also fairly strong in many of us. This process model gives a way into communication but once well into the interaction it is likely to be more complex than the model can usefully handle. In practice it means people may be approached in the following ways:

Person 1 (quietly). 'Hello, would you like a quiet stroll around the garden?' (silence.)

'Isn't that a marvellous bush?' (silence.)

'It's so peaceful here away from the traffic,' (silence.)

'I wonder if you have had any thoughts about that proposal I put the other night?' (Quadrant 2.)

Person 2 (warmly). 'How lovely to see you. How are you feeling? You're looking really relaxed these days. I want to talk to you about something that is really exciting me, and I would enjoy it very much if you could work with me on it. Let me explain it to you.' (Quadrant 4.)

Person 3 (seriously). 'Hello. I've had another idea about that matter we were talking about last night. This is it,' (explains).

'Do you feel that's worth following up? You may be a bit tired after last week's crisis. How do you feel about it?' (Quadrant 1.)

Person 4 (loudly). 'Hey, Bill. Great to see you – good excuse for a drink. Let's push through the crowd to that seat over there. You get a really good view of the river there. Now, how are you feeling? You're looking a bit down.' (Quadrant 3.)

Of course the skill is in correctly deciding what kind of person you are talking to, which is easy with people you know, and not that difficult with others if careful observation and the principles of the model are combined.

What the model enables us to consider is what we actually say to one another after we've said hello.

THE ORGANISATIONAL CONTEXT

We can apply the model just as well to organisations.

Active/withdrawn organisations

Organisations which have the characteristics of quadrant 1 (active/withdrawn) present two diagnostic pictures.

One could be a rather obsessional place that seems to concentrate on memos, structures, rules and procedures, rather like the Apollo organisation described by Charles Handy (1979).

The other is characterised by fear and suspicion. Everyone feels they need to watch their backs. The atmosphere is one of distrust, and information is used as a weapon to be hoarded, manipulated or distorted. It is akin to the paranoid personality.

In both the obsessional and the paranoid aspects, organisational development requires interventions in the thinking mode. A careful analysis of the problem, isolating trends and assessing options, is a necessary preliminary to addressing the problematic emotional climate and the impoverished or injurious interpersonal processes in the senior management team and other groups. As a final stage, the source of greatest resistance, behavioural change, can be addressed, though it would need to be done with deliberation and often a lot of backtracking and re-thinking. Rapid changes and hasty decisions would be anathema to this kind of organisation (see **Figure 33**).

Figure 33: The active/withdrawn organisation

Organisation type	Organisation characteristics	Personality characteristics	Order of intervention
Obsessive (responsible workaholic)	Concentration on rules, procedures etc.	Conformity, inhibition, responsibility, tension, perfectionism	Thinking ↓ Feeling ↓ Behaviour
Paranoid (brilliant sceptical)	Fear, suspicion, covert communication	Rigidity of thought, sharpness, grandiosity, keeping on top of things and people	

Passive/withdrawn organisations

The passive/withdrawn organisation of quadrant 2 is comparatively rare. The process of operating at work, even to minimal requirements, would generally take employees out of this particular adaptation. There may be some specialist libraries, museums, or research bodies which exist in this kind of rarefied state but very few.

Those that approximate to it would be characterised by great self-absorbtion, limited contact with their environment, and low levels of interaction or communication internally and across boundaries. There would be a sense of detachment, avoidance of contact, little exchange of emotions or feelings.

Interventions would be at the behavioural level of joining them very unobtrusively in their activity, then moving to the thinking mode. Working with feelings would be experienced as engulfing (see **Figure 34**).

Figure 34: The passive/withdrawn organisation

Organisation type	Organisation characteristics	Personality characteristics	Order of intervention
Schizoid (creative daydreaming)	Absorbtion in tasks, low level of communication	Self absorbed, daydreaming, shyness, pleasant and kind but detached.	Behaviour ↓ Thinking ↓ Feeling

Passive/involving organisations

Organisations having the characteristics of quadrant 3 (passive/involving) also present two diagnostic pictures.

One is the anti-social organisation which has a great deal of, and need of, conflict, excitement and drama and a low tolerance of frustration. There will be a lot of energy which can give the impression of a charismatic or glamorous place, but there will also typically be manipulation, aggression, callousness and irresponsibility. It is close to Handy's Zeus type of organisation (1979).

Interventions need to avoid the thinking mode which is commonly an invitation to fight, but instead do things alongside the members to create a friendly, even playful, rapport. When this is established, it may be safe to address group processes and feelings before finally engaging in thinking strategies.

The second sub-type is the passive/aggressive organisation. In this place the members are sitting on a lot of suppressed resentment, and most typically expressed by the stance of 'see if you can make me'. For example, a response to employing consultants might typically be, 'So we called in this group of experts, and I ask you, they didn't tell us anything we didn't already know. They spent two days diagnosing the problem and we got nowhere at all.'

In such an organisation, the management and other groups will say they can't when they can and 'I don't know' when they could know. Working in a college like this is very frustrating because behind the passiveness one senses there is the energy and creativity which, if it could be harnessed, would be invaluable.

Intervention strategies need to focus first on gently confronting the behaviour and then sensitively working with the feelings. This may take time to establish the state where individuals can begin to communicate more.

Typically there is little intimacy in their work life, and employees frequently report a feeling of being cut off from other sections. If they can be wooed to this point, and they do need a lot of attention and appreciation, they can be engaged in thinking about their issues (see **Figure 35**).

Figure 35: The passive/involving organisation

Organisation type	Organisation characteristics	Personality characteristics	Order of intervention
Anti-social	Conflict, drama, opting out of responsibility, aggression	Selfish, charming, callous, articulate, manipulative	Behaviour ↓ Feelings
Passive-aggressive	Isolation, lack of intimacy, paralysis by criticism	Obstructive, stubborn, lonely, resentful	↓ Thinking

The active/involving organisation

The organisation that can be described as active/involving reflects the hysterical personality. These organisations are characterised by over-enthusiasm, high energy, excitability and creativity, with a tendency to over-dramatise and be self-centred. A stereotype might be a theatre company or a performing arts section of a college. Strategic interventions would concentrate firstly on dealing with all the stored-up feelings; and then working with the energy from people airing their emotional responses to situations, to strengthen the bonding between people within groups. From that point it is easier to generate fun and creativity as a way of addressing issues via the thinking processes needed to solve them. The area of greatest resistance is usually in agreeing a course of action, and then getting on with it. This is not the target for first contact (see **Figure 36**).

The Paul Ware model (1983) of personality adaptations is also a useful metaphor for organisations. We may be able to make effective initial contact with management teams and other groups and have greater understanding of the culture within which they operate. Each individual employee may, however, have his or her own adaptation pattern which is different to those of the organisation, and the consultant will need to be flexible in intervention strategies to move between the individual, group and organisation.

Figure 36: The active/involving organisation

Organisation type	Organisation characteristics	Personality characteristics	Order of intervention
Hysterical (enthusiastic reacting)	High commitment, high energy levels, personal interaction, lower levels of planning, drive and task achievement	Over-enthusiasm, self-centred, creative, over-dramatised, excitable	Behaviour ↓ Feelings ↓ Thinking

CHAPTER 12
GAMES

Games are transactions between people which are always destructive to at least one of the players and leave behind feelings of being not OK. They are compulsive and repetitive. People play the games over and over again. Why do people engage in them?

Games provide a number of rewards for those taking part. They satisfy our rackets – that is, they enable us to feel justified in feeling stupid, angry, incompetent or whatever our racket is. We can often satisfy our racket at a superficial level by the practice of 'racketeering'. We can engage with someone in exchanges that let us experience the racket feeling at a relatively light level. Such exchanges might be round the themes of isn't it awful, they're all the same, or aren't we useless. The transactions are at a complementary level and there is no manipulation such as is always found in a game. We are involved in pastiming, not games playing. When racketeering does not work for us, for whatever reason, we are likely to switch into a game.

Games also reward us by reinforcing our particular life position. They provide us with a lot of strokes of the kind we want – and for some players these are negative strokes.

Games pass the time and thus avoid the need to spend it more constructively, for example in intimacy or withdrawal, which may be felt as threatening.

Games have a pay-off in terms of some existential problems the player has.

Games playing is most easily explained by examining it in operation. We give six examples here.

GAME ONE

A lecturer comes in to the head of department's office looking worried.

Lecturer: 'I wonder if you can help me? I've got a real problem.'

HoD: 'Of course. Just sit down and tell me all about it.'

Lecturer: 'I've been teaching for six months now and I'm still making a mess of it. I'm just not making it as a teacher.'

HoD: 'Why don't you apply for an in-service course for teachers at Garnet College?'

Lecturer: 'I'd love that, but my wife is pregnant and I don't want to be away from her more than I have to for the next four months.'

HoD: 'Well, how about the evening sessions the professional tutor is organising on teaching methods?'

Lecturer: 'Most evenings are really tricky for me just at the moment.'

HoD: 'You could read some of the books on teaching. They might help.'

Lecturer: 'Yes, but I don't learn easily from reading things in books.'

HoD: 'Why don't you go and talk to Jim? He's a very skilful teacher, and I'm sure he would be willing to help you.'

Lecturer: 'I've thought of that but what works for him wouldn't work for me.'

HoD: 'Well ... why don't you take a tape recorder into class? You could play it back and find out where you're going wrong.'

Lecturer: 'I don't think I'd be at ease with the machine going.'

At this point the head of department runs out of ideas. He can do one of two things but neither of them will do any good as he is well and truly hooked into the game.

Firstly he could say: 'I don't know. I can't think of anything else to suggest.'

'Well, I guessed you wouldn't be willing to help me.'

The head feels a sense of failure and criticism from his lecturer, so he feels bad. The lecturer feels that if he doesn't get any help when he asks for it, it is not surprising that he is not teaching well, so he goes away confirmed in his racket of incompetence. He can carry on being bad and not take any responsibility for improving.

The second variation the head of department could try is: (angrily) 'Look, I keep on making suggestions and all you do is dismiss them. You've got to get a grip on yourself or you'll never make a teacher.'

'There you are, you see. Whenever I come to get help all anyone can do is get angry with me. How can you expect me to teach well?'

The lecturer goes away feeling justified in his incompetence. He has manoeuvred the head to appear unsympathetic to his problem and the head of department is feeling bad.

This game is known as the 'Why don't you – yes but', and is very common in organisations. The following are the points to notice about it.

The lecturer starts by hooking into the Nurturing Parent of the head. If he cannot do this the game will not work so he will only play this with someone with a strong Nurturing Parent. Games always require two players, and the initiator will look around for a susceptible person. Once found, the game will be played over and over again in various forms.

There is a stage in every game when there is a cross over. Roles change and the knife goes in. In the above example it occurs when the HoD runs out of ideas and moves either to Adapted Child or Controlling Parent. This is what the lecturer is waiting for. He quickly moves into Controlling Parent and leaves the scene.

The lecturer goes away not only feeling legitimate in his failure, but also with an important pay-off – that he need take no responsibility for his performance. The most common kinds of pay-offs in games are avoiding responsibility, avoiding intimacy and avoiding the consequences of one's work (copping out).

Games are very stroke-rich. In the example the lecturer received a a lot of attention and concern fulfilling a need for strokes.

The way to avoid being dragged more than once into this game (almost everyone falls for it the first time) is to keep a firm check on your Nurturing Parent and respond to the initial hook by an Adult statement such as:

'Could you come back tomorrow at 10 o'clock with some ideas of what methods you might find useful, and we can discuss them?'

The HoD will not be bothered with this player again. The last thing the player wants is a solution.

One additional method of analysis is the Karpman Triangle (see **Figure 37**). This identifies three game roles - that of Victim, Persecutor and Rescuer. In most games at some stage there is at least one switch of roles, which may take the unsuspecting partner by surprise. In the above example, the starting position was that the lecturer was a victim and the head of department a rescuer. At the end of the game the victim had moved to persecutor, and the rescuer, possibly first through the persecutor role ended up the victim.

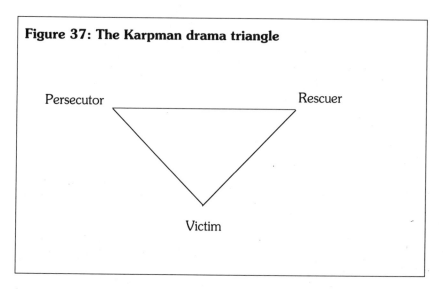

Figure 37: The Karpman drama triangle

Persecutor

Rescuer

Victim

GAME TWO

A course team leader comes into the vice-principal's office.

VP: 'We have to have this course submission ready very quickly. Sorry about it but the committee have been onto me. When is the earliest you can get it done by?'

Team leader: 'If we cut all the corners and I work over the weekends I can let you have it in two weeks.'

VP: 'Two weeks! Far too long. I can't wait that long. I must have it in seven days. If not, believe me, heads will roll.'

The team work very hard on the submission but still haven't finished after seven days. The vice-principal then sends for them and demands angrily why they haven't finished. She goes on to describe a whole series of faults, failings and unsatisfactory characteristics the incompetent and lazy team leader has and discusses with him/her a whole series of undefined threats.

This is a simple version of the game known as NIGYSOB (Now I've got you son of a bitch). It consists of setting someone up to knock them down. In this case by giving an impossible task and then attacking them for failing. It can equally well be set up by giving ambiguous or conflicting instructions, or changing the rules part way through. The pay-off for the vice-principal is that she can legitimately satisfy her anger racket and feel that the failures are not her responsibility but the fault of the subordinates. This game can only be played with someone prepared to take the Adapted Child role, and who needs to be kicked in order to satisfy her racket and so can go away feeling hurt, a failure, guilty or whatever her particular racket is. This is a complementary game in that a NIGYSOB player is looking for a Kick Me player. When the two meet they will cherish each other. The last person the NIGYSOB boss should ever want to sack is her Kick Me subordinate. The game could be easily broken when the vice-principal suggests an unreasonable timetable. The response might be:

'I'm sorry. I cannot do it in seven days and you will have to accept that. I will finish it in 14 days but no sooner.'

Whatever the vice-principal's response, she will realise that she does not have a player for NIGYSOB.

GAME THREE

This is a game which normally takes place over a period of time. A head of department has made a very favourable impression since his appointment a few months ago. He has worked very hard, often late into the evening and has several schemes at various stages of completion for improving the range and quality of the department's work. One of his teachers goes sick for several weeks and he takes her classes. He sits on several committees and has never turned down a request by the principal that he involves himself in some new body. He is also in the middle of working for his MSc via a thesis on management. When one of the vice-principals goes sick, he volunteers to take some of his planning work. Everyone sees him as a dynamic hard-working man for whom future promotion is inevitable, although many wonder how he does it all. Then, just before one of his schemes comes to completion, his thesis is written and his application goes in for the vice-principal's job, he collapses. Over-work the doctor says and orders him six months' rest. He was a great chap and worked like fury, say his colleagues as they pick up the bits of his schemes, course submissions, committee work, and the like. No one criticises him, everyone regards him highly.

Yet he is playing a game, the purpose of which is to enable him to legitimise copping out, and failing to deliver. He is a person frightened of responsibility and of having to be accountable, so he makes sure he never has to complete tasks. In the process he gets many strokes and can legitimately feel he is a highly competent person who would have achieved great things if only it had not been for his breakdown. This is a common game among business executives, some of whom work hard to get their heart attack. It can also be played in a small way with selected projects such as the running of a conference. It is a difficult game to deal with but, if recognised early enough, colleagues can refuse to allow that level of over-work where they have the power.

This game is a version of 'Harried'. Avoidance games (copping out and avoiding responsibility or accountability) have several manifestations.

GAME FOUR

Jeanette was a brand-new lecturer. She had worked in commerce for a few years and had now become a teacher in the business studies department. On her first day she met her head of department, a 35 year old, blue-eyed, rather narcistic man. He made a point of coming over to her and purred, 'It's a delight to have you join us and I will be delighted to spend some time with you to find out some of the interesting things you did before you came here - Oh and by the way I'll, of course, be here to help you.'

For a few weeks, Jeanette had no need to bother him. She noticed he spent most of his time with three of the section heads, and they often went off to the pub together after work. She eventually came up against a problem with a student that she did not know how to deal with, so she went to find the head, locating him sitting and joking with two of his close associates.

She smiled, and said appealingly, 'Excuse me interrupting, James, but I've got a problem in one of my classes I'm not sure how to deal with. I wonder if you can give me some help?'

Her attractive appearance that day triggered off in James some familiar but only half-conscious feelings of jealousy, anger and fear.

In his most condescending voice, he replied: 'Not now, Jeanette. I can't drop everything just this minute. See me later. Check with my secretary.'

Taken aback, all Jeanette could do was to make an undignified retreat.

This is a game known as Rapo and in its social form is a sexual encounter consisting of a come-on, then an indignant put-down when the other person responds. For example, in the above case, James is secretly quite affronted that Jeanette has not sought him out before, so when she does he gets his own back, and reinforces his belief that women try to get their way by seduction. It is of course a type of NIGYSOB, and if Jeanette continues to respond to bogus come-ons and gets put down, she would be playing the Kick Me game. In fact Jeanette never went back to James for help, even though as her head he was paid to give it. This was the pay-off for him. It is a game that can be used to avoid responsibility and keep those who might make demands on you at a distance. It also confirms his belief that all new teachers, particularly women teachers, are useless. It enables him to legitimise his feelings of self-righteousness and annoyance. It hides the frightened child that feels it cannot cope if it really has to operate in the adult world. James, deep down, is terrified of talented and attractive women who might destroy his comfortable world at work.

If a Rapo player can find a complementary victim who comes back over and over again, the victim can be reinforced in her view that nobody helps, people cannot be trusted, those who appear friendly are always going to disappoint you, and so justify her failure to make close relationships. It is also for her a confirmation that it is alright to fail because the people who ought to help her never do, so it is not her fault. In this game James starts as a rescuer and moves to become a persecutor. Jeanette moves further into the victim role. However, in its social setting, the victim can move to rapist or murderer, and the persecutor becomes, very literally, a victim.

GAME FIVE

This is a common game in organisations. In its simplest form it consists of a person performing poorly in some way or other, and when challenged, justifies herself by saying, 'What do you expect from a person with a wooden leg,' (or some other problem or defect)?

As we are likely to feel sympathetic and maybe a little embarrassed about a disability, we make allowances for the bad performance and clean up the mess ourselves. In fact, of course, having a wooden leg does not make any difference to the capacity of the person to maintain high levels of performance. The game player has hooked the other's Nurturing Parent by playing up the victim role. It is another game which enables a person to cop out of performing to reasonable standards and feel justified in doing so.

The wooden leg can be transformed into many things, as suits the person. They may blame their colour, race, sex, age, marital status, education, bad heart, ulcer and so on.

Of course any of these groups (black people or women for example) can and do suffer real discrimination and can legitimately voice that publicly. This is authentic behaviour. The game is the manipulative use of those characteristics we have which might be the cause of discrimination or difficulty. We use them to avoid situations and responsibilities that we could manage perfectly well, often making other people feel guilty in the process.

The antidote for those who notice the game is being played is to recall all those in the organisation who are in similar situations and who do not connect that to a reduced level of performance.

GAME SIX

The final game analysed here is given in its social version, and readers might enjoy looking for parallels in their own organisation.

Two partners, Ann and Victoria, are sitting at home one evening. Ann initiates the game by a series of non-verbal signs – grimaces, sighs, pouts and chain-smoking.

Victoria: 'What the hell's the matter with you tonight?'

Ann: 'None of your business.'

Victoria: 'If you're in one of your stupid moods tonight, I'm clearing off to the club.'

When Victoria returns some hours later, she faces angry recriminations but gives as good as she gets.

Ann: 'What time do you call this? Who have you been with all this time?'

Victoria: 'Don't shout at me! If you make it worth staying at home I would. It's you who drives me out.'

Ann: 'If you cannot see what was worrying me you're even more insensitive than I thought.'

Victoria: 'You've been unbearable ever since your mother came to stay last month, the stupid cow.'

Ann: 'Don't talk about my mother like that – and while we're on the subject, what about your brother? About as tactless as you and twice as ugly.'

At some stage one of them storms out slamming the door and makes for the bedroom.

This game, appropriately called Uproar, requires both participants to be in angry Child leading to Controlling Parent and back. If either go into their Nurturing Parent or Adapted Child in its submissive form, the game will not work. Although it looks like a straight row, it is in fact a contrived game which is played repetitively, and there is no danger of the participants splitting up. They need each other. Their problem is that they want to live together but have difficulty handling intimacy. Therefore, they have to set up situations which enable them to get apart from each other. Like all games, it passes the time in a relatively safe way, and it is very stroke-rich, initially via negative strokes but full of positive strokes when they make up.

In the literature on transactional analysis, many games are listed and described, mostly with examples from social or domestic situations. Readers can imagine for themselves what is involved in organisational versions of the following:

- Games from an initial position of Persecutor;
  blemish,
  courtroom,
  if it weren't for you.
- Games played from an initial position of Rescuer;
  what would they do without me,
  I was only trying to help,
  they'll be glad they knew me.
- Games played from an initial position of Victim;
  see what you made me do,
  stupid,
  schlemiel (creating havoc).

Although the major roles taken may appear to be Persecutor or Rescuer or Victim, in the course of the game players may switch positions, and even then end up where they started, so as to confirm their existential position.

AVOIDING THE GAME

The key tactic is not to collude with the game player. Whatever response you give it must not be one that buys into the game. Almost any other response will be effective in breaking the game, but given that the game player is always working from the Adapted Child state, moves from the Adult or Free Child are particularly valuable in sharply confronting the player.

For example, in the game of Wooden Leg, a response from Adult rather than the intended Nurturing Parent might be, 'Tell me specifically how your wooden leg stops you from marking assignments on time? I am interested to know.'

A Free Child response might be to go into absurd exaggeration. 'You've got a wooden leg! I've got three – all with woodworm!'

The trap is to respond by blaming or from your Controlling Parent because the response can almost certainly be worked into the game. For example, a reply such as, 'You shouldn't play on your wooden leg so much. Haven't you seen all those marvellous people with wooden legs completing the London Marathon?' will push the game player further into a not-OK adaptive state. Martyrdom and put-downs are what they are partially seeking.

The situation might be appropriate for a straightforward exposure of the racket, the game, or the pay-off, such as, 'What I'm observing is that you are inviting solutions to your problem so that you can find something wrong with them all and so do nothing about it. I am not prepared to get involved in that.'

'I feel you are setting up situations so that you can get angry with other people's apparent failure. Do you think that is what you are doing?'

'I notice you invite people to come to you for help and then reject them when they do. You have just done that to me. I am puzzled by what you get out of it. Is it that you don't want to be involved with their work?'

Of course if the other person knows games theory, you can simply call the game, or say 'I see you are game playing. I am not joining in.' No one can guarantee that the response of the player will be constructive, but it is very likely he or she will not try to hook that person into that particular game in the future.

CHAPTER 13

TIME STRUCTURING

The ability of the human psyche to maintain coherent ego states seem to depend upon a changing flow of sensory stimuli. In structural terms these stimuli are necessary to assure the integrity of the neo-psyche [Integrated Adult] and archeo-psyche [Archaic Child]. If the flow is cut off or flattened into monotony, it is observed that the neo-psyche gradually becomes disorganised. (Eric Berne 1975 p83. Authors' additions in brackets.)

The intolerance to long periods of boredom and isolation give rise to the concept of stimulus hunger and it is this which lies behind the idea of structure hunger and recognition hunger. It really does lead to the question of what do you say after you've said hello?

Structure hunger is addressed by each of us in the way we structure our time, because it is on the basis of this that we receive the flow of stimuli and recognition (strokes) that are so necessary for our biological, emotional and psychological well-being.

WITHDRAWAL

Withdrawal is a form of non-contact with the environment. It can be either a rich source of internal stimuli (daydreaming, fantasies, revisiting old memories) or it can lead to a severe deprivation of external validating stimuli, and result in depression and anxiety.

RITUALS

Spontaneous recognition of another person, a glad smile, an embrace is an intimate form of contact, very real and rich. However, other forms of recognition have tended in most cultures to become ritualised, for example the handshake, the enquiry after one's health and so on. So another form of structuring time for a particular kind of recognition is through ritual. It is predictable and recognisable and creates a sense of safety. Most groups, sub-cultural groups, religious organisations, companies, school sports teams and cultures all have varying degrees of rituals. So indeed do families.

PASTIMES

Developing from greeting rituals is social programming called pastimes which take the semi-ritualistic discussions of commonplaces such as the weather, possessions, current affairs or even family affairs. Reminiscence comes into this as does anything that is not directly related to the here and now.

ACTIVITIES

Activities are what we commonly recognise as work, whether paid or unpaid. It occurs when a person's energy is directed to external sources such as tasks, ideas, chores and hobbies.

Activities are a rich source of strokes both from the satisfaction of a job well done and the pleasure of working with other people.

GAMES

A psychological game is an on-going series of complementary transactions leading to a well defined predictable outcome. Games are a way of maintaining the person's view of the world (frame of reference). Games have the capacity for producing large quantities of intense strokes that are mostly negative.

INTIMACY

Intimacy is the most risky, and at the same time the most rewarding way of structuring time. It is the meeting of a person's true self with another. In such contact there is a quality which is instantly recognisable. It feels genuine, true with no ulterior motives or exploitation. However, although it is so rewarding it means taking a risk and 'dropping a front' and is therefore far less predictable. This is why so many people avoid it, particularly if they have any doubts about their sense of OK-ness.

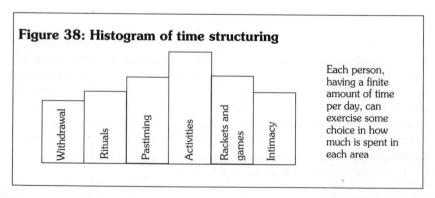

Figure 38: Histogram of time structuring

Each person, having a finite amount of time per day, can exercise some choice in how much is spent in each area

The way in which individuals structure their time will lead us to experience them in particular ways. For example, people who are always pastiming, may be experienced as rather shallow, and those who spend most of their time in activities as rather intense and serious, perhaps even dull.

Some individuals spend a great deal of time in games. The play 'Who's afraid of Virginia Woolf' is a good example of a relationship based on such a pattern. People who habitually structure their time in this way are experienced as manipulative, difficult, unpredictable or exploitative. People who risk intimacy regularly come from a position of I'm OK you're OK and are refreshing, daring and sometimes experienced as childlike because of the large element of trust. **Figure 39** shows how the various ways we structure time can be related to our functional ego state.

Groups also develop personalities which derive from how they spend their time. Some meetings, sections or groups never seem to get down to anything because they are so busy pastiming with 'ain't it awful'. Others are so engrossed in activities that they never seem to observe the niceties of rituals before they begin and members can feel exploited. Other groups reach what Tuckman (1965) calls the performing stage where there are high levels of intimacy and well defined rituals, time for pastiming and lots of productive work. It is also possible for such a group to tolerate silences (withdrawal as opposed to activity on one's own).

Some organisations have roles that foster long periods of withdrawal. In the field of engineering, progress checkers, although involved greatly in activities, can become very stroke deprived and separate from other members of the production team due to the isolating nature of their job. In colleges, the departmental secretary can become very isolated or be the absolute hub of everything. In one college the departments located in the main building had a dreadful arrangement where each secretary, later designated administrative assistant, was housed in a little glass fronted office with no outside window, directly outside the office of the HoD. They were not in the centre of things and only saw people if they had an appointment with their boss. Thus they spent a great deal of time in activities, but reported a growing sense of isolation and stroke deprivation, although not using those words. In stark contrast, those secretaries located in the art department which was in a different building and those located in annexes, enjoyed their jobs, were involved with staff and students a lot more, and spent more time in intimacy and pastiming. They reported loving their work. Many of them felt autonomous, made decisions and felt a real sense of ownership of their department. Their relationship with their head of department was collegial. It clearly depends on the individuals as to whether they abuse such a system, as some certainly will. Others got the work done very efficiently, ran a 'tight ship' and still had time to talk to staff and students about personal issues.

Figure 39: The role of different ego states in time structuring

	Controlling parent	Nurturing parent	Adult	Free child	Adapted child
Withdrawal	Silent self criticism	Silent self-comfort meditation	Thinking about what cities are along the Exeter to Paddington line (for example)	Singing to oneself	Frightening fantasies
Ritual	Taking the children to school/church	Tucking the children up in bed and reading to them	Watching the evening news	Nightly tickle match or pillow fight before retiring	Obligatory annual church service
Pastime	'Isn't it awful?' (about kids, inflation etc.)	'Isn't it wonderful..?'	Exchanging non-essential information ('Did you read about..?')	Telling and knowing jokes	'If it wasn't for him.'
Activity	Supervising others' work disciplining employees	Making beds, bathing the children, giving time to a colleague with a problem	Framing a budget	Playing squash	Doing chores
Rackets/games	'NIGYSOB' 'Blemish' 'Rapo'	'I'm only trying to help you' 'Cavalier' 'happy to help'	No games	No games	'Poor me' 'Kick me'
Intimacy	None	None	None	Sharing, love, joy or pleasure	None

Adapted from Woollams and Brown (1978)

Sometimes what appears a misuse of time can be very productive. For example, a personal recollection. A colleague, of whom I was always rather critical, was always to be seen in the coffee bar or in the corridor talking. This person went off on maternity leave and I was asked to take on her duties, which included timetabling and organising servicing between departments. I went into the office and worked and worked, phoning, leaving messages, writing notes. Finally I decided to block out some time and spend the day on the main site at all the watering holes, to see if I could finalise arrangements.

It was a success, as far as anything like this can be, prior to the start of a new term with so many unknowns, and I realised just how effective the pastiming had been for my colleague. She had networked so effectively that she had completed the task far faster than I had, and I suspect, much more enjoyably.

This incident put me in mind of the origin of Lloyds the underwriters meeting in coffee houses, and tales my father told me of saving thousands of pounds of clients' money over a pint in a City pub.

Many of us , however, have been so imbued with the Protestant work ethic that we may feel such use of time is not acceptable in the workplace. Each has its place – too much of any one will have its effect on the team.

The health of any organisation will be a direct function of the way in which the time is structured. Organisations with a great deal of intimacy will be solicitous of people's well-being, and will be able to work in a co-operative rather than competitive way. There will be more of a sense of community (see Scott Peck **The different drum: community making and peace** (1988) and getting on with the task in hand will be handled most effectively. Competitive organisations will avoid intimacy, may tend to spend more time game playing, as well as in activities. Organisations which have failed to bring about a bonding process with their workforce (Kohlreiser 1990) are more likely to find their staff less motivated and spending proportionately more time pastiming. Pastiming is a safe way of exchanging strokes, but is not goal centred, so the college or company can suffer as a result.

Overall most of us would recognise in ourselves the need for withdrawal, the need for activities, the need for pastiming, rituals and intimacy. We all recognise the feeling when we have slipped into a game, and with more awareness we can begin to recognise the situations (or discounts) that trigger them off. We can recognise that as it is true for us, so it is for the organisations in which we work.

CHAPTER 14

DISCOUNTING

WHAT IS DISCOUNTING?

Everyone will have heard and used phrases identical or very similar to the following:

I can't help it.
What do you expect from them?
It'll be all right in the end.
No point in making a fuss.
I always get lost at this point.
He's so stupid.
They're all the same.
My wife (husband) doesn't understand me.
I must be thick or something.
You look a sight.
They're too busy.
Everything is going wrong.
This is impossible.
We're helpless.
You'll never get that right.
No good complaining.
They always get you in the end.
She's got no feelings.
I don't know what to do.
I can't choose – you do it.

What is common in all these phrases is that either I deny my power (to do anything about it) or your power, or any chance of the situation allowing us any choice. These statements all deny our own capacities and resources. They pretend that an explanation is sufficient if it denies that we or others have the capacity to exercise our skills to achieve what we want. It is a way of giving away our power so that we are losers.

None of the above statements are true. They are all lies – and when we lie about ourselves, others or the situation, we are discounting.

DISCOUNTING BEHAVIOURS

Discounting is something that happens inside us, though it may lead to a spoken statement or some behaviour. I say something to myself which disempowers me to use my resources to deal with what is at hand. Commonly the statement has the element of grandiosity – it is an absurd and grandiose claim of impotence, e.g. he never thinks about me, I can't trust anyone, everything I do is a failure. The behaviour which accompanies internal discounting is generally a form of passivity. There are four main types which can best be illustrated by example.

Doing nothing

In a training workshop the trainer introduced an exercise. She stated that anyone who did not want to do it could move to the side and sit down. Otherwise everyone was to go and find a partner. One man neither moved to the side nor went to find a partner, but just waited helplessly, and as there were odd numbers, he was left at the end as the couples paired off. He looked around helplessly waiting for someone to come and rescue him.

Over adaptation

Two people are detailed to run a workshop session. One arrives to find the other sitting at ease drinking coffee and chatting. He notes the room they are going to use is still unprepared, so takes his coat off and gets down to chair-shifting and other arranging, thinking it's always like this working with her.

Agitation

A member of staff is sitting in a committee meeting which is being badly run with members constantly wandering off the point. He gives more and more physical signs of irritation – shuffling in his seat, sighing loudly, shaking his head disbelievingly, drumming his fingers on the table, shuffling his papers and, when the meeting closes, getting up and stalking out impatiently.

Incapacitation and violence

A working team is given a new, exciting but very challenging programme. One member starts getting headaches and missing team meetings. His health seems to be breaking up, as he takes to his bed more often. The team carry on without him, all working a bit harder to compensate for his absence. Eventually, the manager calls him in and tells him his record is such that he is no longer useful on the team and he is being transferred to another job with fewer prospects of promotion. He is furious, goes out to a series of pubs, and ends up smashing up a bar.

Commentary

In each of the four incidents, there was no attempt made to use personal resources to tackle the problem. Had there been no discounting, the person in the first incident would have either sat down at the side or gone and found a partner. If he was left on his own, he would ask the trainer what she proposed to do about having odd numbers. In the second incident, the person could ask his co-worker whether she had arranged for the room to be prepared, and if not, how they could do it together. In the third incident, the disgruntled committee member could positively intervene in the meeting to bring it onto track. In the fourth, he could have talked to the team about his worries of being able to respond to the challenge and tackled the things he could do. If he was demoted, he could organise a plan for his future career to achieve what he wanted. All the actions actually taken did nothing at all to deal with the problems.

Discounting is endemic and is often difficult for the person doing the discounting to notice – it is so worked into her everyday thoughts and speech. When in driver behaviour, in rackets or in games, or if one or more of the ego states has been de-commissioned, discounting takes place. Go back over the last 24 hours and list as many of your discounts as you can. Note whether you were discounting yourself, someone else, or the situation. For example:

'I always get lost at this point' – discounting my own ability;

'You'll never get that right' – discounting your ability;

'This is impossible' – discounting the possibilities in the situation.

The discount matrix

When we discount we don't tackle the problem. If we could systematically find a way of preventing discounting, we would be improving our problem solving capacity. One particularly useful way of doing this is by means of the discount matrix, developed by Mellor and Sigmund (1975).

It assumes that all discounts can be classified according to area, type and level.

Area

The three areas in which we can discount are self, others and the situation, as already mentioned above. It is the other two classifications that are used in the matrix.

Type

The three types of discounting are stimuli, problems and options. Let us suppose that a teacher is discounting herself by performing poorly, one of the symptoms being the late return of marked work. If she does not recognise that she is returning work late, she is discounting the stimuli.

If she does recognise it, but doesn't think it important, she is discounting the problem.

If she knows it is a problem but doesn't feel she can do anything about it, she is discounting her options.

Level

The four levels or 'modes' of discounting are existence, significance, change possibilities and personal abilities.

Suppose that everyone had gone home early and left me, yet again, to finish everything off.

I could discount the existence of my tiredness and behave as though it did not exist. I would be discounting the stimuli at the level of existence.

I could be aware that it created a problem for me but consider it was so minor it did not matter. So I discount the problem at the level of significance.

I could think of ways of avoiding it in future, by going early myself, and leaving it to the others, but also say to myself that in practice, responsible people don't do that. So I discount the options at the level of change possibilities.

I could say to myself that I would solve it if I could tell the others to stay, but that I haven't the nerve to do it. So I discount the options at the level of personal abilities.

The discount matrix (see **Figure 40**) combines all the possible combinations of level and type of discounting.

The important point is that discounting of ourselves, other people, or situations, is very common. It disempowers us and takes away our opportunity to use the abilities we have to change things for the better. Understanding and overcoming discounts is therefore a crucial skill in our personal and professional lives.

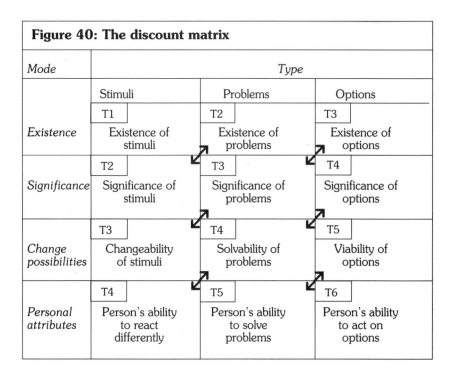

Figure 40: The discount matrix

Mode	Type		
	Stimuli	Problems	Options
Existence	T1 — Existence of stimuli	T2 — Existence of problems	T3 — Existence of options
Significance	T2 — Significance of stimuli	T3 — Significance of problems	T4 — Significance of options
Change possibilities	T3 — Changeability of stimuli	T4 — Solvability of problems	T5 — Viability of options
Personal attributes	T4 — Person's ability to react differently	T5 — Person's ability to solve problems	T6 — Person's ability to act on options

EXAMPLE OF A DISCOUNT

A newly promoted member of staff is totally unaware of the unhappiness around her. Colleagues are grumpy, frustrated and often stop talking as she comes into the room (stimuli). So, she discounts the existence of stimuli (T1) (see **Figure 41**).

Later, as the weeks pass by she begins to notice, but brushes it off by saying to herself, 'It's just them, it's an off day,' and so discounts the significance of the stimuli and the existence of the problem – i.e.

T2

Figure 41: Discounting matrix: level 1

Mode	Type		
Existence	T1 Stimuli	T2 Problem	
Significance	T2 Stimuli		

'No problem,' she says as she continues to behave in much the same way.

After a while she notices that her colleagues are friendly to one another, invite each other to lunch and remember birthdays. She becomes aware of the changeability of stimuli which, in turn, leads her realise there is a problem and it could be about her – she often feels left out. However, she realises that there are options (T3) and different ways of relating to people (see **Figure 42**).

Once this discounting has been acknowledged the new member of staff has to address the way she discounts her ability to react differently. She might say to herself, 'They'll have to take me as they find me, I've always been like this.' If she does, she will automatically discount the solvability of the problem and the significance of the options. If, however, she decides she can learn to stroke her colleagues sensitively, she will discover that the problems with

Figure 42: Discounting matrix: level 3

Mode	Type		
Existence	T1 Stimuli	T2 Problem	T3 Options
Significance	T2 Stimuli	T3 Significance of problem	
Change possibilities	T3 Changability of stimuli		

her colleagues' grumpiness and frustration may well change as she opens up a channel of communication with them. She can become increasingly clear about which options, in terms of her behaviour, are significant to the solution of the problem (see **Figure 43**).

Figure 43:Discounting matrix: level 4

Mode	Type		
Existence	T1 Stimuli	T2 Problem	T3 Options
Significance	T2 Stimuli	T3 Significance of problems	T4 Significance of options
Change possibilities	T3 Changability of stimuli	T4 Solvability of problems	
Person's ability	T4 ...to react differently		

Figure 44: Discounting matrix: level 5

Mode	Type		
Existence	T1	T2	T3
Significance	T2	T3	T4
Change possibilities	T3	T4	T5 Viability of options
Person's ability	T4	T5 ...to solve problems	

She may, at this point, stop herself by saying something like, 'Well, I know all about strokes now, but I just don't think I can do it.' She may still be stuck with parental introjections which tell her, 'Don't make personal remarks.' If she discounts at this level she automatically discounts the viability of the options (T5). (See **Figure 44**)

If, however, she takes the final step and no longer discounts her ability to act on options (T6) she effectively gets herself off the discount matrix and solves the problem. She can do this by practising stroking with one or two people whom she trusts and then can try it out in the work situation. The result – a new level of communication, difficulties discussed and (we hope) invitations to lunch follow (see **Figure 45**).

Figure 45: Discounting matrix: level 6

Mode	Type		
Existence	T1	T2	T3
Significance	T2	T3	T4
Change possibilities	T3	T4	T5
Person's ability	T4	T5	T6 ...to act on options

The discount matrix shows where the person is stuck, i.e. at what level they are discounting. For example, in one college a member of staff, Eric, had been given rapid promotion in the department. He began to cause annoyance to others by making judgements and decisions on areas of work in which he had no special competence. The head of department, Trevor, became aware of this but initially tackled it at the wrong level. Eric did not recognise the significance of the stimuli, i.e. the annoyance of the other staff and therefore did not accept there was a problem. So Trevor's attempts to discuss some options for different behaviour with Eric were a waste of time. He needed to tackle Eric's discounting of the significance of the stimuli before anything else could be done.

In unhealthy organisations the level of discounting is generally very high, whereas those organisations with a healthy ethos move across the discount matrix and thereby solve their problems. Projection, i.e. putting the difficulty wholly onto someone else, is an effective way of blocking problem solving. Sadly it happens all too often and leads to discounting of personal abilities to see and act differently.

CHAPTER 15
DRIVERS

INTRODUCTION

In early childhood we are frequently faced with worrying, frightening or confusing situations which are caused by the adults around us, and which we do not understand. There is not much that we can do to change this directly, because we are so powerless in a world of powerful people. We experience various kinds and intensities of bad feelings, and look for ways of getting out of those feelings, so that we can feel good again.

The adults who relate to us do not deliberately try to create confusion and bad feelings in us. They are doing the best they can to give us the basic understanding and equipment needed to survive in the world. The thousands of messages we take in during our childhood help us to understand the following:

- good standards to work towards;
- ways in which we should be reliable and able to be depended on;
- how we should help other people;
- how we should make good use of time.

These are all key decisions about the kind of a life we are going to lead, and as children we receive much advice and modelling which help us come to these decisions.

However, either because we misunderstood the messages, or because the messages were faulty or contaminated, we may have fundamentally changed their nature, and we see them as a condition for love or approval or even survival – that if we do certain things or behave in certain ways, we will be looked on more favourably and receive positive strokes. The child will decide that:

- I will be OK if I am perfect, then I will be loved;
- I will be OK if I am strong;
- I will be OK if I please you and everyone else;
- I will be OK if I try hard;
- I will be OK so long as I hurry up.

These are known as the five **drivers**. They are compulsive behaviours, and almost all of us have at least one that is well-developed and possibly another relatively strong subsidiary one. We learn in our childhood which of these drivers seems to achieve the particular effect we want.

It is important to differentiate between useful learning about the need to have good standards, to be dependable, to be punctual and to use time well, to put some effort in and not give up easily, and to respect other people's needs; and the compulsive behaviour that must be done in order to feel valued. It is a difference between real choice about standards and powerful compulsions.

DESCRIPTION OF THE FIVE DRIVERS

Be Strong

Behaviour in this driver can cover a number of aspects.

A person can be driven by the feeling that she is tough enough to handle anything that comes along. There is nothing that will find her out or break her down.

Alternatively a person can be driven by the the the feeling that he is above such weaknesses as emotions. He is the tough impassive person, hard as a rock, and apparently without feeling.

Another person may be driven to take charge of or assume responsibility for everything going on around her. She is strong enough to look after everyone and everything.

Yet another is driven by the need to be totally independent. He wants to deal with everything on his own, does not need other people, and is uncomfortable being dependent on anyone.

Finally, yet another person may be driven by the need to be in total control not only of herself but of everyone around her.

Although there will be some differences in behaviour between the sub-divisions, we can generally say that Be Strong people tend to avoid verbal and physical intimacy, they are not open and trusting, and they avoid vulnerable situations at all costs. They make a virtue out of pain, suffering, discomfort and overwork, assuming it is good for the soul and strengthens character. They place great importance on control, particularly over their own feelings, and are often taciturn. It is likely that they have received strong messages in the past such as don't be a child, don't have fun, and don't feel. They probably have strong feelings of rejection and find close intimacy difficult, maybe because their parents were never close to them either physically or emotionally. They are often committed rescuers. In their bad moments they often feel unappreciated in spite of all the strength they give to others. A final pay-off feeling is often extreme loneliness and rejection.

Be Perfect

There are a number of sub-types of this compulsion. One person may be driven by the need to be absolutely clear and precise in everyt˘ing she does, with no possible room for ambiguity. Her normal conversation sounds like an official letter. For example, 'I will give careful consideration to the points you have just made, and when it is clear to me which course of action will lead to the best results.....'

Another person may try to cover every possibility so that nothing is left out or left in doubt. 'On the one hand you can take this view, at least if you can establish any of the following alternatives as viable, though if any of them is not correct you will be in error, unless you are correct in spite of erroneous assumptions because of other factors. On the other hand...'

This is a person who describes exactly what is happening with no interpretation or comment. He never uses metaphors, nor makes qualitative judgements or speculations.

Another person may keep very quiet because if she says or does something it might be wrong. She will not risk making a mistake. There is also the person who is always judging others by picking up the errors and illogicalities in what they say or write, often on very trivial points. He will not let anything pass without putting it through a rigorous critical check.

Yet another sub-type may judge everything rather like the chairperson of an arbitration panel. She waits until everyone has spoken their piece, then delivers her judgement in measured and certain voice. It may or may not be approving, but it will always be patronising.

Finally, there is the person who must complete everything he does perfectly, so he never lets it go. There is always something more to improve or polish up. The end result must not have the slightest imperfection, and so is often never finished.

The Be Perfect person's behaviour will vary somewhat depending on which sub-type is strongest, but in general such people use long words and sentences, and get involved in debate and dispute on almost any issue, however small. They will introduce a lot of qualification and will commonly comment on or redefine a question rather than answer it. They get impatient with other people's imperfections, and dislike any kind of shoddy or unfinished work. To do enough to satisfy the needs of the job would never be enough for them. Obsessive or compulsive behaviour is common, for example in following precise rituals – being obsessively clean or tidy, not stepping on the lines in pavements etc. Depression is often associated with the Be Perfect driver.

Hurry Up

This is typified by people who cannot keep still, talk hurriedly and frequently interrupt others, often finish other people's sentences for them, always seem in a rush, and are inclined to panic. They never seem to live in the present. Their mind is always focused on some point in the future that they want to get to. In a lecture room they are thinking of how they will get home, at home how they will process their work the next day, in front of them is an endless sequence of tasks they must rush to get on with. The injunction from their childhood seems to be don't think, and there is a tendency towards hysteria, sometimes resulting in a total freezing and inability to do anything at all. Often Hurry Up people make a mess of things.

There are two significant points to make about the Hurry Up driver.

Firstly it is important to know whether a person is hurrying away from, or hurrying towards, or just hurrying aimlessly as his typical driver behaviour. One Hurry Up person may be anxious to be away from where she is, checking her watch from the moment she comes in. Another is always anxious about where she has to be in half an hour's time, and can never settle because of this worry about the future. The third person just hurries about anxiously, almost as a conditioned response.

The second and more crucial point is whether a Hurry Up person typically messes things up and loses out, or whether she does get where she is going and achieves what she wants. In the latter case she will always arrive much too early for the party or the train, but at least she will be there. Her driver forces her into compulsive behaviour about getting there, but apart from wasting time, she will get through the day without mishap. In the former case she will rush so much she forgets her ticket, leaves the house door unlocked, trips over a kerbstone, runs and catches the wrong bus, and fails to make it to the train or the party.

It is never difficult to spot the Hurry Up person at a meeting. He will arrive early or late and disorganised, he will keep on wanting to get on with everything, he will display closure behaviour of one sort or another well before the scheduled end, and will probably be the first out of the room.

Try Hard

The compulsive behaviour of trying hard at whatever you are doing, and the belief that most people will see you as OK if you are clearly working hard, is a common enough phenomenon, particularly in Anglo-Saxon, non-conformist cultures. The person with a Try Hard driver is not necessarily a loser, though that is the implication in many books on transactional analysis. He or she may well accomplish what they are doing to a reasonable standard. The essence of the driver is that achievement gives no relief, no sense of completion, but rather of loss, for the person no longer has anything to try hard at. So there is an immediate search for something new to tackle; and in the desperate desire not to be left with nothing to do, many Try Hard people will flit from one task to another, never quite finishing any, and obtaining assurance from the fact that there is always something else to do. This driver can be illustrated by imagining two people climbing up a mountain. One is really working hard at climbing up the path, and when she eventually reaches the top, immediately looks onward to where the next summit is and gets ready to tackle that. For her there is always another slope. The second person stops on the way up to look at interesting rock formations, chats to her companion, and on reaching the top sits down with a great sense of achievement to enjoy the reward of a splendid view.

Messages received as a child by the Try Hard person were of the kind, you can only do your best, if at first you don't succeed and the like, and school reports no doubt commonly said tries hard, or must try harder. Try Hard people compare themselves with others or their own past performance on all sorts of dimensions. They think in terms of league tables and mark lists, and are always checking how they could do better. This can result in a feeling of failure, dispiritedness and worthlessness. However hard they try, nothing seems to quite come right.

The activity that is antipathetic to them is to relax, to stand and stare, to do nothing.

Please

This derives from a heavily over-adapted Child ego state, with parent injunctions not to pay attention to and value one's own needs and feelings. Conditionally, feeling good comes from helping other people to feel good. It is the position of the arch-rescuer, and is built around the myths of duty, self-denial, self-sacrifice and saintliness. The underlying parental message is don't be you, and don't leave me, and the typical internal discount is, what I want or need or think does not matter. The two main variants of Please Me are the strong rescuer and the weak doormat. The strong rescuer is very positive in her statements about sacrificing her own needs for other people, and expects recognition and reward for this, playing her games and seeking pay-offs from that position of strength. It very often goes in tandem with a Be Strong driver. The doormat is anxious, apologetic, guilty, and (underneath) probably resentful or hating. He can be visualised as combining Please Me with Try Hard or Hurry Up. At the beck and call of other people, he may feel tyrannised, and in his games he is a Kick Me player. It is difficult for people with this driver to stand up for their own opinions and pay attention to their own needs and feelings. They may become the devoted company servant, but make bad managers. Their speech is punctuated by phrases such as, I wonder if I could…, I'm sorry to bother you but…., would it be all right if I….? They find it difficult to make and stick to decisions. All the time they check that what they are proposing pleases everyone.

DRIVER BEHAVIOUR AND THE MINI-SCRIPT

We move into behaviour which is associated with our driver because we hope by that means to get rid of our bad feelings, but in fact the relief is bound to be very short-lived. People will approve of us if we can achieve our designated goal, but we are always unsuccessful. Failure is written into the operation. If being approved of is conditional on being perfect, being strong, etc., we are never going to achieve it for very long, if at all.

As we experience the impossibility of reaching or maintaining the behaviour we have set ourselves, we have a number of choices of where we can move. We may move back to where we started and wait for events around us to change and so for our feelings to change. There are however three further possible stages one might go through in this mini-script.

The first of these is called the **stopper**, which is another word for a racket. When we realise that our attempts to show ourselves as perfect do not get the approval which we need, either from ourselves or other people, we move into whatever habitual bad feeling we tend to seek when things are not going well for us, and with which we have at least the comfort of familiarity. There is no automatic association of a particular stopper with a particular driver, but there may be a common sense relationship. We might find, for example, individuals who have the following drivers and stoppers:

Driver		Stopper
Be Perfect	-	Feeling guilty
Hurry Up	-	Panic
Try Hard	-	Fear of failure
Please	-	Feeling embarrassed
Be Strong	-	Feeling unappreciated

It should be emphasised however that a completely different set of stoppers could be equally appropriate.

The second stage in the mini-script is that of the **vengeful child**. This is a reversal or a rebellion against the demands of the driver, and again is an attempt to gain some feeling of OK-ness, however temporary and fragile. At this stage of the mini-script the individual gets rid of his bad feeling of not living up to his driver by pushing the blame on to someone else.

The third stage is that of the **final pay-off**. If what we are really seeking is hard confirmation of our basic beliefs about ourselves in relation to our lives, then we may move into this bleak position. For example, we may confirm our belief that nothing we or anyone else does makes any real difference.

The movement through the mini-script can follow three courses on its route between the driver and the final pay-off, and can at any stage break out of the mini-script and return to pre-driver behaviour. This can be illustrated as shown in **Figures 46** and **47.**

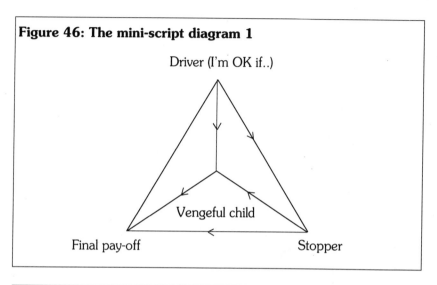

Figure 46: The mini-script diagram 1

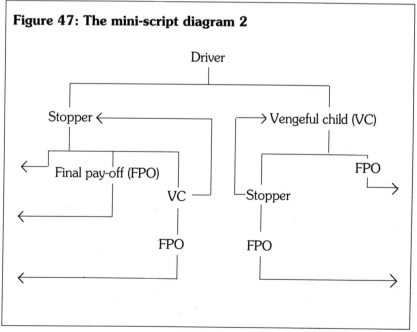

Figure 47: The mini-script diagram 2

Figure 48: Table of mini-script cycle

Driver	Typical stopper	Typical vengeful child	Typical final pay-off
Be Perfect	Guilt	Makes a mess of things	Worthlessness, depression
Be Strong	Unappreciated	Invulnerable to others	Cannot get, nor is worthy of love
Please Me	Misunderstood, embarrassed	Wilfully lacks consideration for others, rudeness	Inauthentic, no one lets me be myself
Try Hard	Fear of failure	I could be the best if I bothered	I'm not as good as I think
Hurry Up	Panic, can't think, tired	Lateness, immobility	Not belonging, craziness

The way in which the mini-script works, often over a very short time, can best be illustrated by examples.

A man with a very strong Hurry Up driver is on a bus to the railway station. He is going for an interview and is anxious to do well as he has failed in his last three job applications. He has therefore rushed his breakfast, dashed out of his house to catch a bus, and sprinted to get on one just leaving the stop. If the bus takes its usual time, he will arrive at the station 45 minutes before his train goes, but he is worried about unexpected events. He sits down breathless but feeling relieved that everything should be alright now. However, as the bus stops and starts along its journey he becomes more and more worried and impatient with each traffic light, each long queue at a bus stop, every slow moving vehicle. Finally the bus gets stuck in traffic at road works and he experiences extreme anxiety bordering on panic that he will miss the train (stopper). As he waits there, he says in his mind to his wife, 'It's all your fault. I wanted to go up overnight. It was you who said there was plenty of time in the morning. It will serve you right if I don't get it – I don't want to go through with the damned interview anyway,' (vengeful child). As he thinks of his lost chances, however, he becomes more and more dispirited, and a feeling of failure in life gradually pervades him (final pay-off). At that point a dog nearly runs under a bicycle and his attention switches to that. That particular cycle of the mini-script is over. In fact he arrives at the station with 30 minutes to wait, and stamps about on the platform impatiently, wondering why he always ends up having to wait for trains.

Another example could be as follows. A housewife believes that she has to have everything done perfectly for her family – the house absolutely clean and tidy, the meals properly cooked and served, etc. (Be Perfect driver). As she becomes totally exhausted after a hard morning of clearing up and preparing for her family's wants and needs, she begins to feel unfairly used by others who take her hard work for granted (stopper). She goes to bed and lies down all afternoon, letting everything go to pieces. The meal isn't prepared, the washing is only half completed and the vacuum cleaner remains in the middle of the sitting room (vengeful child). As her family returns, she comes down and surveys the mess. She thinks, I'm no good at looking after my family. I'm a failure (final pay-off).

CHAPTER 16

RACKETS

RACKET FEELINGS

Everyone feels bad on occasions – depressed, down in the dumps, or upset. We don't, however, feel bad in a generalised way. We express it with a specific bad feeling. We might, for example, feel:

- angry,
- embarrassed,
- guilty,
- frustrated,
- stupid,
- bored,
- clumsy,
- frightened,
- inadequate,
- hurt,
- rejected,
- incompetent,
- anxious, or
- suspicious.

There are other bad feelings described by different adjectives which can be added to this list.

Everyone will have experienced all the above feelings at some time in their lives. But looking at the list very carefully, considering each word and trying to get in touch with the appropriate feeling, one or two of them will, for most people, have a feeling of close familiarity. There will be a feeling there that they really know inside out. They know how it starts, all the different shades and variations and intensities, and how they come out of it. The feeling seems to be triggered by a very wide range of external happenings. This is a person's racket feeling (or feelings – there may be two or even three connected bad feelings).

A racket feeling is a 'favourite' bad feeling. If someone is going to feel bad, then this is the way he or she normally does it because the feeling will at least be familiar and the person will know the worst it can do. To check this out look at the list again and choose the feeling that you experience least often – when you do ever experience that it is much more painful than your racket, because it is almost unknown territory. A racket feeling is a bad feeling which:

- is experienced very often; and
- is inappropriate to the situation.

The second point is important. Feelings which arise naturally out of the situation are not rackety, but sensible responses dealing with the here and now. There are times when it is natural to feel frightened, hurt, anxious etc. But think of the person who seems angry all the time – anything sets her off. Or the person who feels guilty about almost anything – no one else can see why she feels guilty about a particular situation. She seems almost guilty about being alive. Or the person who, in many social situations, no matter how much love or affection is expressed towards her, will feel rejected – these are racket feelings.

THE ORIGIN OF RACKET FEELINGS

Why do people have specific racket feelings? Why those and not others? Why is the man who is always angry not always feeling stupid instead? Why doesn't the woman who habitually feels rejected often feel clumsy?

Racket feelings are learned in childhood. Children are not born with their feelings already programmed towards objects and people. They each learn towards whom and what they can show affection, towards whom and about what to feel guilty, whom and what to fear, whom and what to hate. Although each child will experience all feelings, he or she will eventually adopt a learned feeling which seems to be the most comfortable to hold in an alien situation. The process is complex, not simple, but in essence the child is learning the feelings which best ensure survival in the microscopic world he or she inhabits. Some of the ways these feelings might be generated are as follows. A child who continually hears, 'I'm ashamed of you,' or 'You should be ashamed of yourself,' learns guilt feelings. A child who continually hears, 'You just wait until your father gets home,' learns to feel fear. A child who continually hears, 'Watch out for yourself – don't trust other people,' learns anger or suspicion. A child who continually hears, 'What's the matter with you? Can't you get anything right?' learns to feel stupid.

Another important way a child learns to experience particular feelings is simply to observe what is permitted and what forbidden. In other words, it can model itself on the behaviour of others. When things are bad in the house, if everyone gets short-tempered then this is an allowed feeling the child is likely to copy. On the other hand, being moody may always result in a negative response from adults and the child quickly learns that is not a feeling easily tolerated by others.

PSYCHOLOGICAL TRADING STAMPS

While the child's response and repertoire of chosen feelings might have made sense in childhood situations, they generally continue in adult life long after there is any rationale for them. In their down moments adults tend to seek out situations in which they can re-experience the old childhood feelings. For example, a person who in childhood learned to feel and act clumsy, might as an adult knock things over or drop things so people once more call him stupid. If a person wants to add to her collection of negative feelings, then she will manipulate others to anger her, make her feel guilty, arouse her anxiety etc. She accomplishes this by selectively interpreting what people say, or setting up situations, or playing roles (the inadequate provider or the unappreciated helper for example). Such manipulative behaviour we define as a racket. Each time a person does this we can imagine her collecting a trading stamp and sticking it in her book.

When she has collected enough stamps she can trade them in for a prize – a mammoth piece of self-justified behaviour – from walking out on the job or telling the boss exactly what you think of her, to divorce or suicide. For people who cash in their stamps for these big prizes, the key phrase before the behaviour would be, that's the last straw, I've had all I'm going to take. Many people, however, cash their stamps in regularly for minor prizes of a day off sick, a deliberately spoilt piece of work, or by throwing the in-tray across the room.

OK FEELINGS

Of course much of the time we feel OK, we are not in racket feelings and are not manipulating situations to feed into them. The basis of TA is that behaviour is learned and it can be changed. The essence of psychological growth is to decrease the amount of racket feelings that are reliving the bad experiences of childhood and instead live appropriately in the present.

Note that throughout the above account we have carefully distinguished the use of 'racket' and 'racket feeling'. Many accounts of TA do not do this and this can confuse the reader. So, to summarise, **a racket feeling** is a 'favourite' bad feeling that is repetitive and inappropriate to the situation, whereas a **racket** is a set of behaviours that manipulate the situation or other people so that the racket feeling is experienced.

CHAPTER 17
THE OK AND NOT-OK ORGANISATION

THE NOT-OK ORGANISATION

The not-OK organisation can be identified by a number of clues in behaviour. In not-OK organisations, relations between people are often seriously flawed; relations between the individual and the organisation are mutually destructive.

People go to work to accomplish tasks for which they are paid. We might expect, if we did not know better, that people at work would commonly operate in their Adult ego state, informed by a responsible Parent and the inventiveness, curiosity and fun of the Child. Yet behaviour in organisations seems mostly to derive from those archaic learned states from our childhood, manifested in the functional model as Adapted Child behaviours, some of which are totally incongruous to the current situation. Why should this be? Why is so much time wasted in petty criticisms, minor persecutions, manipulations, apathy, deference and apology – in fact why do we so seldom deal with our bosses, colleagues or subordinates in an Integrated Adult way? This is one of the most important questions organisation theorists can address.

Organisational parenting

At any one time we are negotiating with and trying to survive in a particular kind of world, and the powers of the worlds we encounter, the dramas we walk into as we move on stage, are not something we can shrug off or by which we can remain untouched.

It is commonly accepted that in the first seven years of life the impact of the world that the child experiences and the sense he or she makes of the messages received are the main determinants of script formation. One of the main experiences of the child is the parental messages from powerful authority bodies, most commonly parents or surrogates. These are often interpreted in the light of the child's current intellectual and emotional functioning and may be incorporated into the P1. We experience parental-type messages throughout our lives and we do not acquire just one P1 but an increasing number of P1s as we live through our lives. In other words, we are likely to develop new forms of archaic parental messages and consequent inappropriate behaviours as we encounter situations in which we may define ourselves as relatively weak and an associated body as relatively powerful.

In our society this is particularly likely to happen when we enter the work organisation, though we could also consider it in relation to entering personal commitments such as marriage or partnership. In some cultures it may occur in coming to terms with the state's persecutory power or a very conformist culture or religion.

We can see the process of extra-parenting in its purest form in our work organisations. The organisation is powerful. That is how we most commonly perceive it, and when we enter it and are initially interviewed for acceptance into it, all the symbols and behaviours we encounter reinforce the concept of that power in contrast to our own weak individual presence.

It is the classic parental set-up. The analogy of the baby entering the family and the newcomer entering the organisation can be taken a long way, though it does not fit the fact that we have already probably been through the process before upon entering previous jobs. A more exact analogy would be with the young child being fostered to a series of different homes. As in that case, the new member acquires a set of parental injunctions, commands and permissions, some of which will be wildly inappropriate and all of which will be immature in the sense that they are ingested via the power system, i.e. from the Parent of the organisation to the Child of the worker, and not processed through his or her mature Adult. To deal with the organisation's Parent, the worker develops or reactivates a range of adaptive behaviours. So as old P1 messages are reactivated, the employee will now have an extended repertoire for the Adapted Child. We can note, for example, the adaptive behaviours of employees which they themselves would consider detrimental to their self-respect if engaged outside the workplace – such as deference to managers or collusion with discriminatory practices.

In developing the Parent-Child relationship in the organisation, there are a number of mechanisms operating. A very important one is the motivational drive for affiliation, the need to belong and feel accepted as one of the family. The new entrants will look for ways in which they can establish and cement affiliation, and it is primarily through this process of socialisation that they are brought into the family, learning its ways, norms, culture, special language and rituals. The process of socialisation is one of parenting, or providing models of Nurturing and Controlling Parent introjects, which will tell us what to do if we want to be accepted and get on in the family.

We may also want to please our organisational Parent by our cleverness, dedication to work and usefulness, and look for special notice or praise. In other words we seek to protect ourselves from the greatest fear the infant has – rejection by the family group on which its survival depends. The fact that the grown-up employee has resources and alternatives not open to the defenceless infant may reduce the intensity but not the general thrust of coming to terms with the work organisation. Of course it is not universal. Just as when we were children we operated in our Adult and OK Parent as well as our Adapted Child and archaic Parent, so do employees. Some are able to operate in their Integrated Adult most of the time, but that does not seem to be the common experience.

The process of organisational parenting and of bringing up children works through the stroke economy. The employee seeks to be valued, and looks for concrete signs that his performance and behaviour is accepted. The manager manipulates the use of strokes as does the mother or father with their infant, so that behaviour is conditioned by the fear of withdrawal of love or appreciation. The employee can learn again, as he did in childhood, the experience of unconditional acceptance, strokes conditional on behaviour, strokes conditional on performance – in extreme cases negative strokes for anything, and in stroke-starved organisations the absence of any strokes, which can lead, as in families, to destructive behaviour simply to force a response of some kind. As one experiences stroking, so one learns to stroke – the pattern received by the employee from his superordinates is the pattern likely to be adopted in turn in dealing with subordinates.

The stroking patterns of any organisation are of course likely to be complex and rich. The point emphasised here is that much of the stroking activity replicates the power situation of the infant/grown-up, and is manipulative not only in controlling and conditioning the employees' behaviour and attitude but also in keeping them in a Parent/Child relationship.

If a major driving force is the need for affiliation, and if a necessary expression of this is conscious valuing by others, then it is clear how racket feelings (from part of ourselves that had to develop adaptations in our family of origin) are reactivated when the new employee enters a work organisation. She is likely to feel anxiety, be made to feel stupid or incompetent, guilty or rejected as part of the experience of coming to terms with the work and work groups in the first few days and weeks of employment. Whatever the employee's subjective experience, she is likely to lock the rackets into the relationships with the organisation and its managers, so that for example those with rejection rackets have them amply reinforced by fears of failure to get acceptance or appreciation from their work-group and supervisors. This is likely to be felt whatever the objective reality.

Furthermore, new employees will find their drivers substantially recharged by the experience of coming to terms with their situation. In order to be accepted both by the work force in general and one's own personal work group and supervisor in particular, there will be a power pushing the novice into driver behaviour. The Please Me employee will have full encouragement to make his own needs subservient to others. The Be Perfect employee will look to get her strokes by making sure everything she does is absolutely right. The Try Hard, Be Strong, and Hurry Up employees will be working to get the signals that they are OK with their fellows and supervisors in their own driver-related ways.

Of course we are not arguing that all organisations are in this respect the same. Clearly they operate over a range, from very strong to comparatively mild parenting, and the nature of the parenting also operates over a range from benign to persecutory. The point to establish, however, is that the organisation is a surrogate parent, and the employee experiences parenting in such a manner that he or she acquires a further P1. The employee, like the infant, may react in a whole variety of ways from submission to rebellion. TA used in organisational development programmes can be particularly valuable in working on individual archaic Parent states and can help to develop behaviour from an Integrated Adult rather than Adapted Child in employees.

Management in the not-OK organisation

Up to this point we have looked at the organisation through the eyes of the employee. If we now switch focus to those in management, we can pose a simple question:

Why have you become a manager? What is it about being or wanting to be a manager that attracts you, that reflects your behaviour needs and patterns, that fits into your script?

When the manager is operating from Integrated Adult, she can work productively, fulfilling the necessary functions for which the role exists. The temptations in the managerial position to fall into non-functional and destructive behaviour are, however, very great. It is a superb stage on which to play out script dramas and games, to reactivate rackets, to give or invite negative strokes. The in-built dramaturgy of work behaviour allied to a cast of *dramatis personae* who have different power and status invites the playing out of our various scripts.

In order to test this out for yourself, start by considering the following two questions:

- When, as manager, you are in your not-OK Parent, how specifically do you feel and behave?
- When, as manager, you are in your not-OK Child, how specifically do you feel and behave?

Managers might, for example, feel very persecutory towards their staff, or simply think they are not worth much and make that clear in their behaviour to them. Others might feel that their staff although nice, are not up to the job and need constant help and interference. These not-OK Parent responses are very disempowering for the staff.

Managers might generate feelings of chronic anxiety when in their not-OK Child, worrying about their own competence or popularity, while others might become envious and vengeful towards staff they perceive as better off than themselves in some way.

Every manager will experience not-OK feelings. The important thing is for managers to be aware of their own particular bad feelings, and check they do not use the latitude of their managerial position to indulge in them at their employees' expense.

Managers will become involved in organisational games so a further question is; when you as a manager are in repetitive, gamey situations, are you playing a variant of NIGYSOB or of Kick Me?

It is important for the manager to identify the games he most often plays in order to find avoiding strategies, for they not only waste organisational time but have harmful effects on other people's work. Managers should ask whether they most often take the role of persecutor, rescuer or victim and what effects this has on them and their colleagues. In particular, check what is the psychological pay-off that instigates the gamey behaviour? What is it really all for? Is it to avoid closeness with another organisational member so that behaviour is set up to keep others at a distance? Is it to avoid some part of the work role the manager does not like or is frightened of, so that a repetitive set of actions can ensure she does not have to deal with that? Is it to avoid having to answer for the quality of the final outcome of the manager's work, so never having to take responsibility for what he as a manager is contracted to deliver?

Answers to these questions are likely to lie in the manager's individual script, and it is a useful strategy to look specifically for those script messages from childhood onwards that are about being a manager. What were the messages concerning what a manager was like and what he did? What messages were about power, authority, success, responsibility, order, ambition, command? The best managers carry around very enabling, creative and empowering messages from their past, but many others live out, occasionally or commonly, a script which is harmful to themselves, to those they manage and to the legitimate purposes of the organisation.

THE OK ORGANISATION

The manager in the OK college or organisation recognises and respects the capacity of all the individual members of staff and encourages growth from that strength.

He recognises that organisations do not serve their clients well just because of the cleverness of the manager but primarily because of the commitment and skill of the staff, and the manager's task is to remove all the blocks that prevent such high quality in pursuit of commonly agreed objectives. Managers are in the end at the mercy of the power of the staff. Any staff member, adept as we all are at outwardly conforming to the minimum level defined by the rules, can choose either to work well or indifferently. Choice may be based on many things but significant will be the quality and climate of relationships that the managers have encouraged. If they have encouraged and modelled relationships which are game-free, staff are likely to work well. If, however, they play management games, work from an I'm OK, you're not OK position, establish distance between themselves and main-line staff, emphasise power and status differentials, and use their managerial position to satisfy their rackets, drivers and other parts of their negative scripts, staff are likely to develop various survival responses which will reduce the quality of the college's work.

The manager who chooses to operate from her Integrated Adult state will find opportunities to use all the functional ego states in their positive aspects, and encourage the staff to do the same. She will:

- create a climate of care and give appropriate support and help to staff;
- set standards and encourage the giving and receiving of feedback on performance to these standards;
- expect tough levels of analytic thinking, investigation and decision-making, and demonstrate that herself;
- be sensitive to other people's needs, enthusiasms and idiosyncrasies and be willing appropriately to adapt to them;
- encourage and model creative and intuitive responses in an environment where it is OK to experiment and get it wrong;
- create space for fun and permission for expressing emotion, love and affection, so that it is a part of the experience of organisational life.

The OK organisation will be stroke-rich, and strokes will be a potent mix of unconditional and conditional for the Parent, Adult and Child state. Strokes reinforce the valuing by managers of their staff and the standards which are mutually set and worked for.

The history of the college is acknowledged and respected. It is used as a source of strength from which new decisions can be made, and a developing college encouraged in the direction it needs to take.

CHAPTER 18

PUTTING IT ALL TOGETHER:
A SYSTEMS MODEL OF TA

Many people, when they begin to learn about transactional analysis, seem to have some difficulty in putting together all the pieces of the jigsaw. How do the various concepts, such as rackets, games, ego states, existential positions, and so on all fit together to make a coherent picture? This chapter uses a visual model which shows a linkage and progression, and also suggests where organisational or clinical intervention can be made by the analyst within this system.[1] The model has eight linked parts as shown in **Figure 49**.

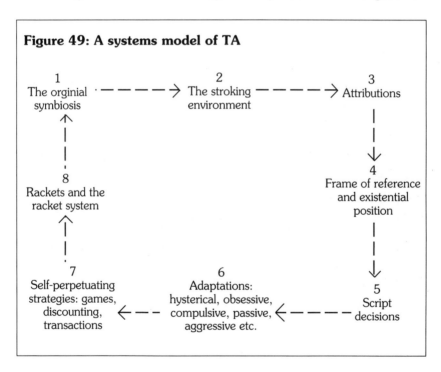

Figure 49: A systems model of TA

1
The orginial symbiosis

2
The stroking environment

3
Attributions

8
Rackets and the racket system

4
Frame of reference and existential position

7
Self-perpetuating strategies: games, discounting, transactions

6
Adaptations: hysterical, obsessive, compulsive, passive, aggressive etc.

5
Script decisions

---

[1] This model was first presented in an article by Julie Hewson, in **ITA News** (1990) under the title *A heuristic systems model of TA*. It deals more fully with its theoretical points and contains full references.

THE ORIGINAL DEPENDENCY RELATIONSHIP

The story starts with the original symbiotic or dependency relationship and the process of bonding that was experienced by the baby. To understand this relationship, we need to know the nature of the family structure, the social and cultural environment in which it operated, the family's attitude towards the conception and birth, and any other important factors at the time. We will get clues to this from:

- the story surrounding the birth;
- the significance of the baby's name;
- any illnesses or emotional disturbances in the family at the time;
- economic hardships or comfort;
- any separation among family members;
- wanted or unwanted pregnancy;
- the health of the mother;
- feeding difficulties both *in utero* and after birth.

Experience as a clinician has confirmed how important it is to pay attention to this kind of information. The following two examples demonstrate this. One client was presenting symptoms of stress. She revealed she had a mother who lost weight constantly through her pregnancy. The client, her baby, was starving at birth and the problem was compounded by unsuccessful breast feeding. This, among other factors, led to extreme agitation around scarcity issues relating to money, work, love and of course food.

Another client, born in an air raid shelter in the second world war, could not understand the terror which surfaced when, in her 40s, she went to Munich to complete her training which took place in a basement flat.

People who experience difficulties on their arrival into the world may be very sensitive to the quality and extent of welcoming when they experience new beginnings in later life.

We can translate this into organisational life. The arrival of a new staff member is a kind of birth and the experience will affect the bonding of the new member to the work team and organisation. Kohlreiser (1990) has brought to our attention the importance of allowing new entrants to establish their identity in this new setting before being defined by their work performance. The issue is further explored in Hay (1991).

THE STROKE PATTERN

The second stage in the sequence involves the transactional analysis concept of strokes. The unique pattern of strokes, given and received, sought for and rejected, positive and negative, is established early in life and then powerfully influences our subsequent experience. Important elements in the individual's stroke pattern are:

- the strokes the child gained for doing at the expense of being;
- the power and preponderance of negative strokes for being and doing, and the child's response to them;
- significant sources of strokes that may have gone against the family trend.

In this second stage the following rules set out by Steiner (1974) become established in the child's mind:
- don't give strokes if you have them to give;
- don't ask for strokes when you need them;
- don't accept strokes if you want them;
- don't reject strokes when you don't want them;
- don't give yourself strokes.

Such rules lead to a loveless or joyless script in later life. Stroke patterns are equally important in organisations. The attention managers give to the quality of strokes relevant to the task, the individual and the life of the team, help to determine the success of the organisation and the health of productive relations within it.

ATTRIBUTIONS

The next link is concerned with attributions; the descriptions which are placed on people that are defining and confining like psychological strait jackets. From our earliest days we have attributions placed on us, which discount the huge richness and diversity of our potential. Some we may welcome. 'You are just like....' can be wonderful if you are being described as your beautiful, kind, talented and fun-loving Aunt Ceinwen, but not so great if it is your Uncle Harry who was a drunk, a waster and never succeeded at anything. At its heart, attributing is a way that other people tell us they know best who we are, what we are, what are our limitations, and the effect commonly is that we negate our own understanding of ourselves. This operates as well in the work organisation as in the family.

THE FRAME OF REFERENCE AND EXISTENTIAL POSITIONS

Through their early experiences, individuals come to make decisions about how life generally is for them, and we can examine this through the TA concept of life positions or existential positions, combining it with the concept of the frame of reference. [2]

The notion of the frame of reference assumes the child, some way or another, comes to make statements like, 'I see that is how it is for me and

[2] The frame of reference concept is taken from the **Cathexis reader: transactional analysis treatment of psychosis** (Schiff et al. 1975).

others, that is who I am, and that is how I am in relation to those outside in the world'. Much of this happens subconsciously and can be a continuing process rather than a once-and-for-all decision.

We can visualise it as follows.

The searchlight illuminates the child's world which to him or her is the totality. They cannot know the team illuminates only 45 degrees or so of a full circle of light. The restriction operates through the mechanisms of exclusion and contamination which we can examine through the structural analysis of ego states.

A contamination is the term given to a situation in which present reality is clouded by fears from the child's past or prejudices from the introjected Parent (i.e. the views of other people ingested whole).

An example of the two would be as shown in **Figure 50**.

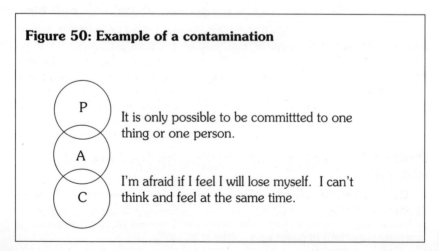

Figure 50: Example of a contamination

P

It is only possible to be committted to one thing or one person.

A

C

I'm afraid if I feel I will lose myself. I can't think and feel at the same time.

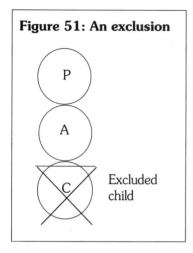

Figure 51: An exclusion

P

A

C Excluded child

An exclusion takes place when a person operates as though they have no contact with their feelings or sensations (exclusion of the Child ego state), or seems unaware of values, morals or shared codes of behaviour (exclusion of the Parent ego state) – see **Figure 51**.

There are four basic life or existential positions.

Position one: I am OK with me and you are OK with me

Those who take this position have a healthy optimistic stance in life. They can freely and autonomously relate to others and can creatively and purposefully get on with their lives.

Position two: I am OK with me, but you are not OK with me

Those taking this position feel OK at the expense of another, and is generally a defensive choice to avoid feeling not-OK oneself. Commonly, the origin is from a parent who modelled the position in relation to the child. It is sometimes called the paranoid position because people who hold it are frequently persecutory or distrustful, but they might equally be over-solicitous and smothering to make recipients feel and appear to be not-OK.

Position three: I am not OK with me, you are OK with me

This is a fundamentally depressive position. Individuals decide that if things go wrong it is all their fault, and if they are not making a mess of things, they will sooner or later, whereas other people seem to be able to handle things. This also is a defensive position, against a deeper anger and belief that they are OK really, and it is the others who are not. However, at a social level (see chapter 7 on Transactions for definition) they apparently operate in the victim position.

Position four: I am not OK with me, and you are not OK with me

This is a position taken by people who have become so desperate as to decide that neither they, nor anyone else, are worthwhile. It is a position of despair, of hopelessness, and is common among employees suffering from burnout.

Any of these positions can be a temporary experience. Certain people or situations may catalyse us into one of them. However, most people appear to assume a basic life position from which they selectively perceive the world. It is though, a choice and what is chosen can be changed. **Figure 52** shows the four basic positions.

Figure 52: The existential positions	
I am not OK with me You are OK with me	I am OK with me You are OK with me
I am not OK with me You are not OK with me	I am OK with me You are not OK with me

SCRIPT DECISIONS

Script decisions occur at any point along the system so far described being placed here on the diagram for ease of visualisation. In fact script decisions can occur at any point along life's journey. Though early transactional analysis literature implied that most script decisions were made in the first few months, it is clearly true that later traumatic life events may also turn a person's view of themselves and the world upside down. Whenever they happen such decisions, to use Eric Berne's analogy, are like bent coins in a pile of pennies which affect the stability of the column above them.

Later script decisions may be in response to new or traumatic events; they may change the direction of a person's life or may reinforce or elaborate earlier pre-verbal script decisions.

In addition, as children grow they hear a range of 'good' parental values passed to them in the form of 'work hard,' 'set high standards,' 'get on with it,' 'show sensitivity to others,' etc. They are the commands or counter injunctions, and these affect the way a child learns to make his or her way in the world. If they are particularly powerful, the child feels driven by them and for this reason Kahler grouped a range of counter-injunctions under five headings which he called Drivers. These were: Be Perfect, Be Strong, Please, Hurry Up and Try Hard (see chapter 15).

When we put these two concepts together, we have the script flowing along at a deeper level, and the counter script the more visible manifestation.

An example would be as follows: as long as I work hard on behalf of others, I have the right to exist. This will be maintained in equilibrium until the needs of others become too demanding or the strain of work leads me to evaluate my life. At this point the script issue of not existing or not taking care of my own needs is likely to surface.

The script is a life plan made outside conscious awareness which informs at some deep level the course of a person's life. The frame of reference is the result of the script decisions, and by selectively perceiving the environment so that it matches the script, leaves whole areas of possibilities and options unexplored. If it is brought into conscious awareness, a person can, if they so choose, change a part or the whole of their script.

Capers and Kahler (1974) developed Berne's original idea that a person's script can be played out over very short periods of time. Second by second, Kahler noted down his subject's phrases, tones and gestures. He noticed, just before they moved into scripty behaviour or feelings, there were certain driver behaviours (see chapter 15).

In essence, once in driver behaviour, a person can play out in microcosm the whole script, hence the name mini-script.

Adaptations

The term is taken from an article by Ware (1983) and reflects the whole philosophy embodied in transactional analysis, namely that people are free to make choices; and although early decisions can be restricting and sometimes very damaging, they made sense to us at the time and were the best we could manage as infants. We should respect even quite extraordinary coping mechanisms and adaptations the child had to make in order to survive early family life. Typical coping mechanisms might be a decision not to say what you mean, or a determination not to experience certain kinds of feelings.

So adaptations are survival mechanisms, and Ware analyses a number of adaptations that explain much of the negative behaviours of the Adapted Child, Controlling Parent and Nurturing Parent using the functional model of ego states.

Once we see the configuration of thought patterns, feeling states, and behaviours as adaptations for survival, we can stop giving them persecutory labels; and instead use them as another way of telling the story of a person's struggle to survive in a sometimes hostile world (see chapter 11 on process communication).

Self-perpetuating strategies

As we live through our life, we spend time maintaining the decisions and positions we have taken, and reinforcing our frame of reference. We use a whole collection of operations to do this. These are our self-perpetuating strategies, and, in transactional analysis language, include the following:

- games;
- habitual ways of transacting;
- time structuring;
- discounting;
- passive behaviours;
- thinking disorders;
- stroke patterns;
- drivers;
- selective remembering;
- selective perception.

An analysis of any of these can show how the frame of reference can be maintained almost indefinitely and outside our awareness.

Rackets and the racket system

What at first sight seems a simple concept, the racket, has been complicated by a number of different definitions:

- Rackets are defined as feelings used to manipulate or exploit others (Berne, Steiner, Goulding and Goulding) ;
- [rackets are] feelings experienced as pay-offs in games, and also the reason for playing them (Berne, Steiner);
- [rackets are] feelings substituted for suppressed or prohibited feelings (English);
- [rackets are] feelings outside the context of the here and now (Goulding and Goulding);
- [rackets are] an underlying exploitable design for experiencing unpleasant feelings (Holloway).

Erskine and Zalcman (1979) developed the racket system as a way of resolving some of these differences They describe the racket system as:

Self-reinforcing and distorted systems of feelings, thoughts and actions maintained by script-bound individuals. It consists of script beliefs and feelings, external displays, internal experiences and reinforcing memories.

Thus racket analysis includes both the internal (intrapsychic) processes and the external associated behaviours related to script.

Referring back to the interview of Frazer and Mona (chapter 4), Mona began to feel bad when Frazer failed to meet her in the way she needed. Within a short time, the following would be activated:

Script beliefs about herself

'I'm not alright. No one ever pays any attention to me.'

Her beliefs about others

'They are alright. They seem confident and so sure of themselves.'

Her beliefs about the quality of life

Disappointing.

The racket feeling

The feeling at the time of script would be sadness. The feeling activated would be anger.

The observable behaviours (rackety displays)

Lack of eye contact, talking faster first and then withdrawing, becoming monosyllabic.

Reported internal experiences

Heartache (literally).

Fantasies

I will end up alone and nobody will love or miss me.

Reinforcing memories

Times when she was excluded as a child.
Times when her sister put her down; hung her up on a peg in the barn and left her there in the dark.
Being unpopular at school.
Husband running off with someone else.

Erskine and Zalcman make the point that 'as a whole, the racket system is maintained through selective awareness and perceptions which are based on requirements of script and involve discounting as a mechanism.' Thus, Mona did not notice the non-verbal strokes Frazer had provided, such as tea and biscuits; she discounted his genuine interest in what she had done over the last academic year, and by her response, she was instrumental in activating in turn his own racket system.

To complete the exploration of some of the concepts underlying the theory of transactional analysis, we now return to the original symbiosis. Observable manifestations in adult life of all that has been discussed so far can be seen in choice and practice of profession or relationships. It is fascinating to discover how what we are doing now in some ways reflects the expectations and patterning we had in early life. So many people in helping or caring positions have found that in order to mitigate against early messages of 'Don't be important,' and 'Don't have needs,' they learned to take care of others. That is how they countered their script and got their strokes.

This awareness of any of the staging posts on the system's circuit and a useful intervention at that point could effectively change the whole system. Strategic interventions can require a new pair of eyes; hence the importance of management consultants.

A SELECT BIBLIOGRAPHY ON
TRANSACTIONAL ANALYSIS

INTRODUCTORY BOOKS

1 Harris, T A (1973) **I'm OK, you're OK.** Pan. ISBN 0-330-23543-5
   A best seller and very readable, particularly the first six chapters. However, the reader should be aware that some of the theory is now seen as a little suspect and further reading is advisable.

2 Harris, A B and Harris, T A (1986) **Staying OK.** Pan. ISBN 0-330-291-36-X.
   A sequel to **I'm OK, you're OK**, it is equally readable and a higher quality book. Basic theory is condensed into the first chapter.

3 James, M and Jongeward, D (1973) **Winning with people: group exercises in transactional analysis.** Addison-Wesley. ISBN 0-201-033-14-3.
   A companion book to **Born to win** and itself serves as a good, simple introduction, but the value of the book is in its exercises, intended to be done in groups, but easily adapted to individual use.

4 James, M and Jongeward, D (1978) **Born to win: transactional analysis with gestalt experiments.** New York, Signet Books ISBN 0-451-081-69-2.
   A best seller, the book contains many exercises with which the reader might not wish to be bothered, but the text itself forms a very clear introduction to TA.

5 Klein, M (1980) **Lives people live: textbook of transactional analysis** Wiley. ISBN 0-471-276-49-9.
   A bit more than an introduction, this book relates TA to psychoanalytic thought, deals with some pathologies in TA terms and gives examples of therapy sessions. Somewhat idiosyncratic in its treatment of theory.

6   Stewart, I and Joines, V (1989) **TA today: a new introduction to transactional analysis**. Lifespace. ISBN 1-870-244-00-1
An excellent introduction covering all major concepts of TA. Challenging and worth working through.

7   Woollams, S and Brown, M H (1979) **The total handbook of transactional analysis.** Prentice-Hall. ISBN 0-138-819-12-2.
A very good introduction, particularly to scripts, but it assumes slightly more of the reader than some others books.

FOLLOW-UP BOOKS

8   Birnbaum, J (1975) **How to stop hating and start loving**. Heinemann. ISBN 0-434-901-46-6.
A popularisation of TA theory that is easy to read and has good examples. Its particular value is its concentration on hostility and anger.

9   Dusay, J M (1980) **Egograms.** Bantam. ISBN 0-553-118-50-1.
A short and very useful exploration of the egogram as a technique for self-examination by one of Eric Berne's collaborators.

10 Haimowitz, M and Haimowitz, N (1976) **Suffering is optional: the myth of the innocent bystander.** Evanston, Illinois. Haimwoods Press. ISBN 0-917-790-01-4.
A short, clear account of TA. Includes a useful question and answer section.

11 Klein, M (1981) **How to chose a mate.** Marion Boyars. ISBN 0-714-527-27-0.
A popular version of her earlier book (Lives people live) concentrating on close relationships. The Driver questionnaire is not, in our view, very reliable.

12 Klein, M (1983) **Discover your real self.** Hutchinson. ISBN 0-091-516-80-3.
Develops a theory of personality and has an extension of driver theory, but readers needs to keep their critical wits about them. Not a book to read unless you have a firm grasp of TA theory.

13 McKenna, J (undated) **I feel more like I do now than when I first came in.** St Louis, Formur.
Don't try to understand the title, ignore the appalling sub-editing and stagger through the bad writing. It has a lot to say about stroke profiles and makes some useful, unorthodox points on the way.

14 Steiner, C (1971) **Games alcoholics play.** Grove Press. ISBN 0-394-478-53-6.
This is a short, well-written and very penetrating book on scripts but particularly concerned with self-destructive behaviour and its accompanying set of games.

15 Steiner, C (1974) **Scripts people live.** Grove Press. ISBN 0-394-492-67-6.
A major book on scripts written by one of the great TA theorists. Highly recommended.

16 Tanner, I J (1973) **Loneliness: the fear of love.** Harper and Row. ISBN 0-060-142-18-9.
This is a short but not necessarily easy book. It assumes familiarity with TA language and thinking. Its value is in its analysis of loneliness and feelings of being unloved.

BOOKS ON MANAGEMENT

17 Barker, D (1980) **Transactional analysis and training.** Gower. ISBN 0-566-021-18-8.
The best of the books in this section and written from an English point of view. It is written from the point of view of a management trainer.

18 Bennett, D (1979) **Transactional analysis and the manager.** American Management Association. ISBN 0-814-4-75-11-6.

19 Meninger, J (1973) **Success through transactional analysis.** Signet.
Its approach may be brash, the style unattractive, and the examples all taken from American business life, but it has some useful points to make.

20 James, M (1975) **The OK boss.** Bantam. ISBN 0-203-032-72-4.
Another book from this prolific stable and a useful standard application of TA to business practice.

21 Jongeward, D *et al* (1976 rev ed) **Everybody wins: transactional analysis applied to organisations.** Addison-Wesley. ISBN 0-201-032-71-6.
Contains some useful detailed examples of the application of TA to business and industrial firms. The contributions vary in interest and quality.

TA AND RADICALISM

TA has generally been seen as a therapeutic way of adjusting people's approach who are at odds with the world. A more radically political line has been developed by a group of psychotherapists on the west coast of the USA under the general inspiration of Claude Steiner.

22 Steiner, C (*ed*) (1975) **Readings in radical psychiatry.** NY, Grove Press. ISBN 0-394-178-68-6.
Read particularly the manifesto and the chapters on principles, alienation and stroke economy.

23 Steiner, C (1981) **The other side of power.** NY, Grove Press. ISBN 0-394-179-26-9.
Not strictly on TA, but developed out of his previous work as an analyst. The subtitle is: how to become powerful without being power hungry.

24 Wyckoff, H (*ed*) (1976) **Love, therapy and politics.** NY, Grove Press. ISBN 0-394-179-06-4
A further collection of essays in the same vein as **Readings in radical psychiatry.**

TA AND FEMINISM

The above three books (22-24) are informed with a generally feminist view and there are a number of specific chapters on women. Read particularly Hogie Wyckoff's chapters on women scripts and the stroke economy, and problem solving groups for women, reproduced in both **Readings in radical psychiatry** and **Love, therapy and politics.**

25 Jongeward, D and Scott, D (1976) **Women as winners: transactional analysis for personal growth.** Addison-Wesley. ISBN 0-201-034-35-2.
This covers some basic TA theory, but then analyses women's role in TA terms. Liberal rather than radical.

OTHER SPECIALIST OR THEORETICAL BOOKS

26 Barnes, G (ed) (1977) **Transactional analysis after Eric Berne: teachings and practices of three TA schools.** NY, Harpers College Press. ISBN 0-061-684-12-0.
A textbook with various authors exploring the state of TA theory, in some cases somewhat scholastically.

27 Clarkson, P (1991) **Transactional analysis: an integrated approach.** Routledge.

28 Goulding, M and Goulding, A (1979) **Changing lives through redecision therapy.** NY, grove Press. ISBN 0-394-179-80-3.
Another of the schools of TA based on script redecisions. An important book.

29 Hay, J (1991) **Transactional analysis for trainers**. McGraw Hill
A very thorough book from a leading practitioner of TA in organisations.
ISBN 0-077-074-70-X

30 James, M and Jongeward, D (1975) **The people book: transactional analysis for students.** Addison-Wesley. ISBN 0-201-3279-1.
Though very similar in approach to **Born to win** and **Winning with people: group exercises in transactional analysis**, it has been written specifically for students in schools and colleges and contains a great many exercises. It is a good quarry for those engaged in teaching TA.

31 Pitman, E (1984) **Transactional analysis for social workers and counsellors: an introduction.** Routledge and Kegan Paul. ISBN 0-710-095-81-3.
The introduction to TA is a bit compressed and perhaps goes too deep too quickly, so there is some ambiguity round structural analysis of ego states. The references to social work and counselling are very relevant and useful.

32 Reddy, M (1980) **Handbook for TA users**. M Reddy.
An excellent book in loose-leaf form with 56 sheets on various aspects of TA, divided into general background material, theory, applications, exercises and training materials, and review and research material. Available from the author: 90, Church Road, Woburn Sands, Bucks.

33 Schiff, JL (1975) **Cathexis reader: transactional analysis treatment of psychosis.** NY, Harper and Row. ISBN 0-060-457-73-2
One of the 'schools' of TA. The application of TA in clinical therapy via Jacqui Schiff's unique approach. Easily comprehensible.

34 Stern, E (ed) (1984) **TA: the state of the art. A European contribution.**
Netherlands, Dorcrecht, Foris Publications. ISBN 90-676-50-36-6.
Essays mostly from Europe on historical and philosophical perspectives, developments in theory, therapeutic communities and schools and work. The tone is theoretical but the general quality is very good.

35 Stewart, I (1989) **Transactional analysis counselling in action.**
Sage. ISBN 0-803-981-90-2.
An important book that all professional counsellors should have.

THE ERIC BERNE COLLECTION

Sooner or later one has to approach Berne's books – later rather than sooner as they are not easy. Berne writes in an elusive, humorous, elliptical and metaphorical style which makes him easy to misunderstand and his crucial insight is easy to miss in the first reading. There is a danger of hero-worshipping him. Not all his books are equally good. The following are necessary to study at some stage.

36 Berne, E (1975) **Transactional analysis in psychotherapy.**
Souvenir Press. ISBN 0-285-647-76-8.
The early exploration of the development of his basic ideas.

37 Berne, E (1963) **The structure and dynamics of organisations and groups.** NY, Lippincott. (Also NY, Grove Press, 1975, ISBN 0-802-100-97-X)

38 Berne, E (1970) **Games people play: psychology of human relationships.** Penguin. ISBN 0-140-027-68-8
A best seller in its day but generally then misunderstood and needs to be read in the context of his other works. Very penetrating on game theory.

39 Berne, E (1975) **What do you say after you say hello?** Corgi. ISBN 0-552-098-06-X.

At his most brilliant and the culmination of his life's thinking. If you only read one of his books this is the one.

ARTICLES

40 Capers, H and Kahler, T (1974) The mini-script. **Transactional Analysis Journal.** Volume 4 Number 1. pp26-42 January.

41 Erskine, P and Zalcman, M (1979) The racket system: a model for racket analysis. **Transactional Analysis Journal.** Volume 9.

42 Kahler, T (1978) Process communications. **Transactional Analysis Journal.** Volume 8.

43 Mellor, K and Sigmund, E (1975) Discounting. **Transactional Analysis Journal.** Volume 5

44 Ware, P (1983) Personality adaptations. **Transactional Analysis Journal.** Volume 13 Number 1. pp11-19

References

Adair, J (1984) **The skills of leadership.** Gower

Berne, E (1975) **Transactional analysis in psychotherapy.** Souvenir Press

Bettelheim, B (1976) **The uses of enchantment: meaning and importance of fairy tales**. Thames and Hudson

Bowlby, J and Fry, M(1985) **Child care and the growth of love**. (2nd edition) Penguin

Capers, H and Kahler, T (1974) The mini-script. **Transactional Analysis Journal.** Volume 4 Number 1 pp26-42.

English, F (1971, 1972) The substitution factor: rackets and real feelings. **Transactional Analysis Journal.** Volume 1 Rackets and real feeling. **Transactional Analysis Journal.** Volume 2

English, F (1977) What shall I do tomorrow? Reconceptualising transactional analysis in Barnes, G (ed) **Transactional analysis after Eric Berne: teachings and practices of three TA schools.** NY, Harpers College Press.

Erikson, E H (1964) **Childhood and society.** Hogarth Press

Erskine, Richard (1991) Transference and transaction: critique from an intra psychic and integrative perspective. **Transactional Analysis Journal.** Volume 21

Erskine, Richard and Zalcman, Marilyn (1979) The racket system: a model for racket analysis. **Transactional Analysis Journal.** Volume 9

Foster, P (1991) Creating a college for adults in Turner, C (ed) **Guide to college management**. Longman

Goulding, M and Goulding, R (1979) **Changing lives through redecision therapy**. Grove Press USA

Handy, C (1979) **Gods of management**. Pan

Hay, J (1991) **Transactional analysis for trainers.** McGraw Hill.

Hewson, Julie (1990) A heuristic systems model of TA. **ITA News**. Number 26 pp2-5. Spring 1990

Holloway, W (1977) Transactional analysis: an integrative view *in* Barnes, G (ed) **Transactional analysis after Eric Berne: teachings and practices of three TA schools.** Harpers College Press

Joines, V (1986) Using redecision therapy with different personality adaptations. **Transactional Analysis Journal.** Volume 16 Number 3

Kahler, T (1978) Process communication. **Transactional Analysis Journal.** Volume 8

Kahler, T (1979a) **Process therapy in brief**. (3rd edition) Human Development Publications

Kahler, T (1979b) **Managing with the process communication model**. (2nd edition) Human Development Publications

Karpman, S (1968) Fairy tales and script drama analysis. **TA Bulletin** Volume 7

Karpman, S (1971) Options. **Transactional Analysis Journal** Volume 1

Kohlreiser, G (1990) Paper presented to EATA Conference in Brussels. [unpublished]

Levin, P (1982) The cycle of development. **Transactional Analysis Journal** Volume 12

Mellor and Sigmund (1975) Discounting. **Transactional Analysis Journal** Volume 5

Peck, M Scott (1988) **The different drum: community making and peace.** Century

Schiff, J et al (1975) **Cathexis reader: transactional analysis treatment of psychosis**. Harper Row

Schmidt, B (1990) Exercises and discussions during a a teaching session in London. [unpublished]

Sharpe, Tom (1978) **Wilt**. Pan

Steiner, C (1971) **Games alcoholics play**. Grove Press USA

Steiner, C (1974) **Scripts people live.** Grove Press USA

Stewart, I and Joines, V (1987) **TA today: a new introduction to transactional analysis**. Lifespace

Tuckman, BW (1965) Developmental sequences in small groups. **Psychological Bulletin.** Volume 63

Ware, P (1983) Personality adaptations. **Transactional Analysis Journal** Volume 13

Woollams, S and Brown, M H (1978) **Transactional analysis: the total handbook.**

INDEX

suggesting 75

symbiotic relationship 160